URGENT
ARCHITECTURE

URGENT ARCHITECTURE

40 SUSTAINABLE HOUSING SOLUTIONS FOR A CHANGING WORLD

BRIDGETTE MEINHOLD

W. W. NORTON • NEW YORK • LONDON

When the cost of projects is given in foreign currency, that cost is the original cost; for the convenience of American readers, it has been converted to dollars at rates current at the time of writing.

For information about permission to reproduce selections from this book, write to Permissions, W. W. Norton & Company, Inc., 500 Fifth Avenue, New York, NY 10110

For information about special discounts for bulk purchases, please contact W. W. Norton Special Sales at specialsales@wwnorton.com or 800-233-4830

Printed in Singapore by *KHL Printing Co. Pte Ltd*
Book design by *Guenet Abraham*
Production manager: *Leeann Graham*

Library of Congress Cataloging-in-Publication Data

Meinhold, Bridgette.
Urgent architecture : 40 sustainable housing solutions for a changing world / Bridgette Meinhold. — First edition.
   p. cm.
Includes bibliographical references and index.
ISBN 978-0-393-73358-7 (pbk.)
1. Housing—Environmental aspects. I. Title.
HD7287.M438 2012
720'.47—dc23   2012012361

ISBN: 978-0-393-73358-7

W. W. Norton & Company, Inc.
500 Fifth Avenue
New York, N.Y. 10110
www.wwnorton.com

W. W. Norton & Company Ltd.
Castle House, 75/76 Wells Street
London W1T 3QT

0 9 8 7 6 5 4 3 2 1

ACKNOWLEDGMENTS

There are hundreds of people whom I have met along my path and who have influenced my life, leading me to where I am today. So if you know me and have spent time with me, you have likely affected me on some level and helped me become who I am. For that I thank you and can only hope I have done the same for you.

Specifically though, I'd like to recognize those who directly helped me through college and my early career. You encouraged me to make a difference and use my "smarts" for good. A wholehearted thanks goes out to Dr. Greg Bailey, my advisor at San Diego State University; Chuck Andraka, my boss at Sandia Labs; Jochen Fuglsang, my boss in Germany at REpower; Gil Masters, my professor at Stanford University; and Richard Young, who taught me a lot about consulting.

I'd especially like to thank my editors at Inhabitat.com: Jill Fehrenbacher, Mike Chino, and Yuka Yoneda, who gave me my start in writing about green design, architecture, and sustainability. They have helped me explore thousands of new ideas and have most certainly made me a better writer. Also, to my readers on all the blogs I have written for—I do it for you, in hopes of inspiring you to design bigger, better, and more sustainably.

Huge thanks go out to my dear friends and family, who have always believed in me and cheered me through life. Thank you especially to my parents, Mike and Kathy, who told me I could be anything I wanted, and to my brother, Casey, for his enthusiasm and support of both my art and writing. Last but certainly not least, thank you to my husband and best friend, Matt, who gave me the courage to follow my dreams and who built me a shipping container art studio in which to pursue them. I never would have gotten here without you.

CONTENTS

PREFACE

As I wrapped up my ideas on sustainable housing for our future world, I was impatiently waiting for the six feet of snow in my yard to melt. In the time that I have lived in Park City, Utah, 2011was the biggest winter I ever experienced and ranks with the record-breaking winter of 1983. The weather was unpredictable and uncommonly strange to say the least. I am grateful, though, to live in an A-frame cabin expressly designed to handle huge snow loads and feel confident that we are equipped to handle above-average years. We are lucky—with a solidly built and durable home and very little to fear in terms of natural disasters other than a small quake or a blizzard.

Most of the world is not so lucky and it is with these people in mind that I wanted to write this book. This last decade has been harrowing in terms of natural disasters, too many even to list. In 2011 alone, we saw multiple large earthquakes, massive flooding, and a catastrophic tsunami that has left a horrible scar, the effects of which we will all feel for years to come. Billions are unprepared for the disasters and changes to our climate that are predicted.

My goal is not to explain the serious threats we will face in the future due to climate change, increasing natural disasters, and our rapidly rising population. Many experts, scientists, and researchers cover these topics in much greater detail and I am grateful for their work. Instead, I want to show that one of the ways we can protect ourselves and save lives is by building better housing. We have the technology and know-how to build stronger, more durable, energy-efficient, sustainable, and disaster-proof housing; we just need to prepare and be smarter with our planning and construction. The shelters and homes in this book serve as examples of what is possible, what is on the market, and what technologies and designs will be able to help us in the future. Certainly there are hundreds of great examples out there; these are just a few that are relevant, interesting, and applicable.

I am not an economist, urban planner, politician, or humanitarian, so I do not pretend to suggest how we actually respond to emergencies or upgrade our housing stock. Rather, this book is intended as a sourcebook of ideas to show that disaster-proof and sustainable homes exist, are cost effective, and are not beyond our capabilities. Hopefully, these shelters and homes will serve as inspiration to architects, designers, governments, and organizations that offer aid in their work, and even to homeowners looking to live more sustainably.

We must be able to adequately provide housing for the masses when disaster strikes, whether that disaster happens in a matter of minutes from an earthquake, through a slow process like rising sea levels, or even because of poverty. If our greatest strengths as humans are innovation and compassion, then we must work to provide housing solutions for those who need them. *Urgent Architecture* explores architectural and design solutions that can help us build for those who need help in the form of safe, sustainable, and healthy homes.

INTRODUCTION

Our world is in flux and seemingly out of control. Catastrophic disasters rock our lives monthly, pollution is rampant, the global population is skyrocketing, and the climate is unpredictable, leaving our future completely uncertain. How then do we find some semblance of normalcy and a feeling of safety in these chaotic times? A natural reaction is to go home, connect with family and friends, cook meals together, and find safety under our roofs. Yet, around 100 million people are homeless and almost 1 billion people live in urban slums with substandard conditions. This means that at least 17 percent of our global population is without even adequate shelter and that millions more live in homes in need of major energy-efficiency and structural upgrades.[1]

Billions of people in this rapidly changing climate are at risk of losing their property, homes, and even their lives because they live in inadequate housing. The world is desperately in need of a major retrofit in how we design, plan, and build homes. We have the technology to solve the problem, but we need to implement these sustainable, renewable, and smart solutions immediately to avoid catastrophic losses in the future.

THE NEED FOR BETTER HOUSING

In 1946, Charles Abrams, a prominent advocate for housing reform to aid those in poverty and founder of the New York City Housing Authority, said, "Housing in the 20th century has been one continuing emergency."[2] The statement still rings true, and now in the twenty-first century we have even more to contend with than just poverty. As the world changes due to rising population, increasing disasters, and climate change, we must prepare and safeguard ourselves from calamity by improving our housing. With secure, more durable, and sustainable housing we can provide for those who need homes, decrease our vulnerability, survive through natural disasters, limit destruction, and adapt more easily to changes in our climate.

Better housing is needed on a global scale and not just for the poor. Though a billion people live in substandard conditions in both developed and developing countries, there are many who are not considered poor but need more efficient, structurally stable, and secure housing. Every person should have the right to an affordable roof over his or her head, as well as privacy, space, security, lighting, heating and ventilation,

OPPOSITE
DRASH convoy in Mississippi to aid relief efforts after Hurricane Katrina. (DRASH)

ABOVE
Flooding in areas north of Rio de Janeiro, Brazil, in early 2011. (ShelterBox)

11

a healthy environment, tenure, water, and sanitation. The housing should be able to withstand extreme weather, earthquakes, and the effects of time. Additionally, everyone should have easy access to his home, work, and amenities, all within a reasonable distance. These are the basic rights that every human should have, and yet many do not. It should be our goal to provide this and more for everyone, whether they are poor, homeless, disabled, refugees, or victims of disaster, regardless of whether they are from developing or developed countries.

Many interweaving factors affect our housing crisis. The following is an overview of the factors causing the continuing housing emergency.

Population Growth

In 2000, global population had just crossed the 6 billion mark and just a decade later it reached 7 billion. By 2030, global population is expected to hit 8.3 billion. Currently about 50 percent of the world lives in an urban location with many forced into slums, and rapid urbanization is expected to increase urban dwellers to 60 percent by 2030.[3] Providing adequate housing for an extra 1.3 billion people, in addition to the 1 billion currently living in slums around the world, is an emergency in itself. This leaves us less than twenty years to build a new supply of housing efficiently and economically for those who currently need it and for those who are expected to be born into this world.

In May 2011, the UN updated its population growth projections: by 2050 global population is expected to exceed 9 billion and by 2100 hit 10.1 billion people.[4] In less than a hundred years, the planet will be a far more crowded place, and efficient and sustainable housing will be absolutely necessary if we all hope to peacefully live together.

Dwindling Resources

Annually, the earth is able to produce only a limited quantity of resources, which is referred to as its biocapacity. As a result of the growing population and our rapidly increasing consumption, global resources are spread more thinly. According to the Global Footprint Network, in 2007 the world had a resource capacity of 1.8 global hectares (gha) per person, but in reality we demanded 2.7 gha per person.[5] This means that on average, each person used more resources than the earth could regenerate in that year. We are quickly blowing through

our resources, polluting what we have, and putting great strain on the earth's capacity to regenerate itself. Biocapacity can also be thought of as an annual budget, and right now we are operating at a deficit.

More people and a limited amount of resources to spread among us means that there are fewer materials to build with, less land to build upon, more food to be produced, and more drinking water to be found or created. Unless we can dramatically increase our resource efficiency and decrease our demand, millions and even billions more people will end up living in slums, without access to safe drinking water, sanitation, or food.

Poverty

Almost a quarter of the world lives below the poverty line, meaning that they have no means to buy or build adequate shelter for themselves.[6] Many of these people live in slums consisting of makeshift shacks that provide little security or privacy and have difficult or no access to clean water and sanitation. With no support, funds, or proper materials, the poor are unprepared to improve their conditions or move somewhere safer. As the population increases, poverty will increase as well,

making the task of providing housing even more challenging.

Conflict

Though conflict and war are nothing new, dwindling resources, increased poverty, and population are likely to lead to an increase in conflict between countries as they fight to gain hold of resources, water, and land. Conflict will put an even greater strain on existing resources and will result in destruction and loss of human life. Conflict often causes refugees to seek asylum in safer locations, where they inevitably need new housing. Hopefully the world can work together to share resources and resist the urge for conflict.

Inadequate Building Codes

Many people, as already noted in the preface, live in substandard conditions without access to basic needs like water and sanitation, but many more live in housing that is considered adequate but that couldn't survive a natural disaster such as an earthquake. When homes are not designed or built to withstand severe storms, earthquakes, flooding, and other forces of nature, lives are lost and destruction is unavoidable. Lax building codes

LEFT
Building the straw bale house.
(PAKSBAB))

RIGHT
A destroyed home after the
Kashmir earthquake in 2005.
(PAKSBAB)

and substandard construction are at the root of many housing problems around the world.

In the last half century, masonry construction has become popular globally and is perceived as strong, but often it is not built correctly. In addition, these newer masonry homes are rarely designed to handle the climate and culture of the given region, resulting in houses that are poorly insulated, are not properly ventilated, lack daylighting, and are structurally unsafe. Without proper reinforcement, foundations, and construction, these masonry houses crumble from earthquakes, are shorn away in landslides, and blow over in strong storms.

Building codes save lives. Take, for example, the difference in damages and lives lost between the Haiti and Chile earthquakes of 2010. The 7.0 M_w earthquake in Port-au-Prince, Haiti, resulted in the loss of 222,500 lives, affected 3,700,000 others, and caused US $8 billion worth of damage. The 8.8 M_w earthquake in Concepción, Chile, resulted in a loss of 562 lives, affected 2.67 million people, and caused US $30 billion worth of damage.[7] Whereas the Chile earthquake was much larger and stronger than the one in Haiti, Chile is accustomed to earthquakes and has implemented more rigorous building codes to

save lives and property. Certainly the cost of the disaster was higher in Chile, but that is because it is a more developed country. Disasters in poorer countries with less stringent building codes may not cost as much, but they often take more lives.

Worldwide, cities, regions, and countries need to create or reexamine their building codes to ensure that safe and appropriate houses are being built. Vernacular architecture is often the best place to start, making use of locally available materials and culturally acceptable designs that are better suited for the climate. Adjustments may need to be factored in to ensure structural stability, but in general, vernacular architecture has evolved over hundreds of years to withstand local hazards and weather. Better building codes and enforcement of those codes will lead to a more robust housing stock and save millions of lives.

Natural Disasters

Natural disasters occur when a hazard such as an earthquake or storm affects the lives of people and causes death, damage, and/or destruction. A hazard is only considered a disaster when it occurs at a site where people live. Natural disasters in the last century have risen exponentially, for multiple reasons: population growth, rapid urbanization, substandard construction, lack of adequate building codes, poverty, conflict— and climate change. It is not necessarily that in the last century more hazards (tornadoes, earthquakes, floods, extreme temperatures, storms, fires, landslides, and so forth) have occurred, but that more people live in hazard-prone areas.

According to the EM-DAT, The International Disaster Database, in the last century deaths have actually decreased over time, which is attributable to improved technologies and early-warning systems. On the other hand, the number of people affected has significantly increased.

ABOVE

Temporary shelters built after the
Kashmir earthquake. (PAKSBAB)

can add up to damages similar to megadisasters like the Haiti earthquake in 2010 and the Japan earthquake and tsunami in 2011. So we must be prepared not only for the "big ones" but also for the small disasters that strike weekly.

Even more frightening is that disasters will occur more frequently as a result of population growth, rapid urbanization, substandard construction, lack of adequate building codes, poverty, conflict, and climate change. As the population expands, we will find ourselves more often in the crosshairs of hazards. The 2000–2010 decade was the deadliest in the last century for natural disasters, and in the ensuing decades, they are bound to intensify. We should expect to see megadisasters regularly and smaller disasters weekly, and it is with this expectation that we must shore up our housing stock and prepare for the worst.

This means we are minimizing deaths as the number of natural disasters increases, but because there are more people located in high-risk areas, many more people are affected. As one would likely expect, the cost of these natural disasters has also shot through the roof.

The last decade has been particularly harrowing, and 2010 was the deadliest year in the last two decades, with the most deaths resulting from the Haiti earthquake (>222,500) and the Russian heat waves (~56,000). In 2010 alone, there were 373 disasters, 296,800 deaths, 207 million people affected, and US $109 billion worth of damage. Whereas 2010 may have been the deadliest, 2005 ranks as the year with the most reported natural disasters (432) and also as the costliest (US $173 billion).[8] Data on disasters from 2011 is still being tallied and calculated, but it is likely to be the costliest year on record. Another factor to consider is that there are hundreds of smaller natural disasters that happen regularly, which

Climate Change

In 2007, the Intergovernmental Panel on Climate Change published its latest report on the causes and effects of climate change. As they reported in their Fourth Assessment Report, the warming of the earth is unequivocal and we can expect to see a rise in global temperatures between 1.1 and 6.4° C (2.0 and 11.5° F) in the twenty-first century. This warming is expected to result in overall rising sea levels, increased warm spells, heat waves, heavy rainfall, droughts, tropical cyclones, and extreme high tides.[9] Climate change will also affect the supply of fresh water, agriculture, and other resources. There is even research that suggests climate change may cause an increase in earthquakes and tsunamis as a result of fresh water melting from the ice caps and redistributing itself across the globe, putting pressure on the faults.[10]

Those living in cities, on coasts, and in developing nations are at a much greater risk due to climate change. Cities will experience higher temperatures than rural areas because of the urban heat island effect. Most of the world's population lives in Low Elevation Coastal Zones (less than ten meters above sea level), where they will be directly affected by the rise in sea level, storm surges, and flooding. We may see large cities and even countries, like small island nations, forced to move inland, buy land from other countries, or adapt to living on the water. Overall, poorer developing nations are at greater risk due to climate change than developing countries, because they have fewer resources with which to prepare and adapt. Climate change may even create refugees who will be forced to migrate and rebuild their lives completely.

A rise in natural disasters as a result of climate change is likely, and one way to reduce our risk is to improve our homes and implement solutions that can adapt to our changing climate. These homes must be built to withstand severe storms, rising tides, flooding, earthquakes, and extreme temperatures. In addition to structural integrity, our homes of the future must be better equipped to provide energy, water, and even food in a sustainable manner. This means that homes should be capable of producing their own energy, collecting and processing water and waste, and

growing their own food, all while having minimal impact on the environment. The goal should be to build self-sufficient, durable, secure, strong, and healthy homes.

The causes of our global housing problem are complicated and multifaceted, and they exacerbate one another, resulting in a negative feedback loop. The only way to break the cycle is a large-scale redirection toward sustainability.

HOUSING SOLUTIONS FOR A RAPIDLY CHANGING WORLD

As result of our rapidly changing world, we must nimbly and efficiently reevaluate our current housing stock and look to solutions that protect us in times of emergency, during recovery periods, and then permanently for a sustainable future. We will see many disasters in the future, and we will have to rebuild to keep living our lives. If we can invest in ourselves by building smarter and preparing for the future, we can hedge our bets against climate change, dwindling resources, disasters, and our rapidly growing population.

We need all sorts of solutions, from those that can help us immediately in an emergency situation to permanent solutions that are built to withstand extreme temperatures, seismic activity, and severe storms. We need emergency and temporary shelters; good-quality but quickly erectable homes; homes for the poor, homeless, and those with low incomes; and finally super-sustainable homes that can provide for us in any climate. The technology is all currently available and we have the skills and techniques to build exemplary homes; we urgently need to put that know-how to good use.

One final note. It's not enough for us to design and build retroactively after damage and loss from disasters. We must also think to the future

and prepare ourselves and our homes for an uncertain climate, both political and environmental. By anticipating variable, extreme, and inclement weather, we can hopefully save ourselves from disaster. Building our homes so they can adapt may save us not only from catastrophe and devastating losses but also from death. There is an urgent demand for nimble, sustainable, and adaptable architecture and we must build in order to survive.

NOTES

1   Gustavo Capdevila. "HUMAN RIGHTS: More Than 100 Million Homeless Worldwide." IPS Inter Press Service, 30 March 2005. Accessed April 2011, http://ipsnews.net/news.asp?idnews=28086; United Nations Human Settlement Programme (UN-HABITAT).
Planning Sustainable Cities: Global Report on Human Settlements 2009 (UK and USA: Earthscan, 2009).

2   Charles Abrams. *The Future of Housing* (New York: Harper & Bros., 1946), p. 346.

3   United Nations Human Settlement Programme (UN-HABITAT). *Planning Sustainable Cities: Global Report on Human Settlements 2009* (UK and USA: Earthscan, 2009).

4   "Global Population to Pass 10 Billion by 2100, UN Projections Indicate." UN News Centre, 3 May 2011. Accessed 15 May 2011, http://www.un.org/apps/news/story.asp?NewsID=38253&Cr=Population.

5   B. Ewing, D. Moore, S. Goldfinger, A. Oursler, A. Reed, and M. Wackernagel. *The Ecological Footprint Atlas 2010* (Oakland, CA: Global Footprint Network, 2010).

6   United Nations Human Settlement Programme (UN-HABITAT). *Planning Sustainable Cities: Global Report on Human Settlements 2009* (UK and USA: Earthscan, 2009).

7   EM-DAT: The OFDA/CRED International Disaster Database, Université Catholique de Louvain, Brussels (Belgium). Accessed 30 March 2011, http://www.emdat.be.

8   Ibid.

9   "IPCC 2007, Summary for Policymakers." In M. L. Parry, O. F. Canziani, J. P. Palutikof, P. J. van der Linden and C. E. Hanson, eds. *Climate Change 2007: Impacts, Adaptation and Vulnerability. Contribution of Working Group II to the Fourth Assessment Report of the Intergovernmental Panel on Climate Change* (Cambridge, UK: Cambridge University Press, 2007).

10 B. McGuire. "Potential for a Hazardous Geospheric Response to Projected Future Climate Changes." *Philosophical Transactions of the Royal Society A: Mathematical, Physical and Engineering Sciences,* 28 May 2010. Accessed 9 April 2011, http://rsta.royalsocietypublishing.org/content/368/1919/2317.abstract.

ABOVE
The exterior of the home is clad in charred wood, which is a natural way to preserve the wood. (I See For You / Föllmi Photography)

1.

RAPID SHELTERS

A basic shelter that can be assembled in less than a day to provide protection from the elements for a limited amount of time.

Pop-up, emergency, temporary, survival, homeless, and rapid—all words that describe the most basic of shelters. Whether needed after a natural disaster, during a search and rescue mission, or to last through the night in harsh conditions, rapid shelters are survival tools. These shelters are designed not for permanence but for their ability to quickly provide warmth, shelter from the elements, and some semblance of security against insects, animals, and other people.

Unfortunately, after an emergency rapid shelters are often used far longer than intended. Days turn into months and sometimes even into years. Victims of natural disasters use their plastic sheeting and makeshift, found material shelters much longer than they should have to. Their use may be intended for days, but they need to be durable enough to last for years. Cost is of course a critical element in the design of rapid shelters, and keeping the cost low is certainly ideal, but the more durable the design, the more times it can be reused in other emergency situations.

The features of a shelter help determine the specific situations for which it is best suited. For example, the operation of a search and rescue team's base station is best served by a reusable and very sturdy shelter. Likewise, when a natural disaster occurs in a place with limited resources, long-lasting emergency shelters are optimal and may need to be shipped into the area. Design and use of rapid shelters should take into account the following elements:

1. **DEPLOYMENT:** Consider the location of the emergency, shipping method, mode of transportation, and overall weight in order to minimize delivery time and cost.

2. **ASSEMBLY TIME:** Assembly should be quick; the unit should be ready for use in less than a day.

3. **SKILL LEVEL AND TOOLS:** Users should need minimal skills and tools to assemble the unit.

4. **COST:** Overall cost of the unit for manufacturing, delivery, and assembly should ideally be kept low.

5. **DURABILITY:** Shelters must be able to withstand local climate and long-term wear and tear.

7. **SECURITY:** Users need security against insects, animals, and other people.

8. **REUSABILITY:** The ability to reuse the shelter multiple times increases its longevity and usefulness, thus justifying cost and materials.

This section presents various examples of shelters that can be assembled in less than a day, some in a matter of minutes— everything from flat-packed huts to inflatable pop-up units and even shelters created from natural materials. When time is of the essence in an emergency situation, low-cost shelters should be immediately accessible and quickly assembled with few tools and the most basic of skills. Once erected, the shelters should provide security and protection from the elements, last for more than a year, and be reusable in other situations.

PROJECT NAME
HabiHut
(http://www.thehabihut.com)

LOCATION
Camp Jacmel, Haiti

PROJECT TEAM
Eldon Leep, Bruce Leep,
Dave Kraft, and Ronald Omyonga
through HabiHut

ARCHITECT
Bruce Sterling

**PARTNER
ORGANIZATIONS**
The Umande Trust
(http://www.umande.org)
and The Haiti Hut

PROJECT YEAR
2011

PROJECT AREA
118 square feet

APPROXIMATE COST
$2,500

PHOTOS: HabiHut

1.1

Habihut

Flat-packed, hard-sided plastic shelter, installs in less than an hour, providing security and a durable shelter for the interim; has also successfully been used as a water kiosk in developing countries.

Tents are very useful in postdisaster situations. They can be quickly deployed and rapidly set up and have a relatively low cost point. Conversely, they are very flimsy, break easily, provide no security, and cannot last through a strong storm. For a shelter to be of any help immediately after a disaster, it needs to have the rapid deployment qualities of a tent but the long-lasting qualities of a more permanent shelter. HabiHut is trying to fulfill both of these needs with their hard-sided plastic panel shelter. Flat-packed for efficient and fast transport, HabiHuts can be assembled by a few people in under an hour. The resulting shelter provides greater security, durability, and weather resistance than a tent.

The idea for the HabiHut started back in 2008 when Bruce Sterling, an architect from Aspen,

Colorado, came up with a shelter concept that was based on a three-sided pyramid. The inherent strength of the design prompted Eldon Leep and his team to further develop Sterling's idea and fabricate prototypes. The HabiHut has a hexagonal footprint, a three-sided roof with three windows, a door, and a skylight. Constructed out of polypropylene sheeting with aluminum framing, the structure is able to withstand physical impacts and high winds.

After the earthquake in Haiti in the spring of 2010, two HabiHuts were installed; they have lasted through many storms, whereas less sturdy shelters were blown down. In early 2011, twenty HabiHuts, funded by the United Way, were sent to Camp Jacmel near the Haitian town of Jacmel to help provide housing for more than three

thousand people living in the area. The units were erected on concrete pads, which provide a solid foundation. For the remainder of 2011, HabiHut, in collaboration with their Haitian partner, HaitiHut, expected to deliver fourteen additional units to Haiti, some of which would be used as shops and kiosks.

HabiHuts are manufactured in Bozeman, Montana, and then flat-packed along with all the parts and pieces into a single box. If a large shipment were requested, seventy-two units could be loaded into a shipping container for efficient delivery. Each HabiHut weighs less than 400 pounds and can be quickly assembled in a couple hours with minimal labor and tools. The lightweight shelter is almost 12 feet tall at the inside apex and can easily be moved by a few people, if necessary. The high-density, UV-resistant polypropylene copolymer panels come in a variety of colors, don't crack, peel, or fade, and are double-walled for a small amount of inherent insulation. A single door and operable windows can be opened to permit ventilation, but also locked to provide security when the residents are

gone or asleep. A skylight and vent in the three-sided roof bring in more natural daylight and let hot air escape. When assembled, the waterproof shelter is anchored down to immobilize it against strong weather or earthquake.

The shelters are expected to last from ten to fifteen years, thanks to their durable plastic panels and aluminum frame, and could even be reused many times. Broken parts can easily be replaced, and everything can be fully recycled at the end of the shelter's life. HabiHuts' hexagonal footprint allows multiple units to be joined together to create larger structures as needed. The shape also creates a spacious interior and multipurpose areas within a single room.

Originally the shelter was intended only for housing, but the design team has expanded the concept to use the huts as water kiosks—a community service that also supports the local economy by selling drinking water to villagers. In collaboration with The Umande Trust, HabiHut's first project installed eight shelters in a village outside of Nairobi, Kenya, in the summer of 2009. Around a year later, three water kiosks were installed in Nairobi, Embu, and Kiserian, a town twenty miles outside of Nairobi. These kiosks are equipped with a 1,500-gallon water tank, faucets, solar panels, two lights, and a mobile phone charging station. They provide villagers with clean drinking water as well as a place to charge their phones, as many do not have access to grid-sourced electrical outlets.

LEFT

Rendering of HabiHut, front panels invisible.

RIGHT

HabiHut village at Camp Jacmel, Haiti.

Additionally, the kiosks create a number of jobs and a modest income.

In 2011, a local water company began testing the Kiserian kiosk as a pilot project in hopes of minimizing illegal water connections. If the project is deemed successful, more water companies will buy and install these inexpensive structures. An unexpected benefit of the kiosks is that the solar-powered lights stay on until around 10 P.M., greatly improving security around the kiosks. HabiHut is also collaborating with Fenix International, a San Francisco–area tech company, to source the charging stations, which use either the sun or human power via a bicycle to generate power.

The water kiosks seem to be successful in their trial runs, so hopefully there will be more interest on the part of water companies in Africa and around the world to set up these microbusinesses. HabiHut is working on deploying a "Village in a Box," which would contain enough materi-

als for fifty shelters and water and toilet kiosks to provide for a village of 250 people. They are currently working with the Umande Trust to find a location for this village and hope to complete it in 2012. Now that the HabiHut has seen some action in the field and the team has improved upon their design, the hope is to increase manufacturing so that thousands of units could be stockpiled around the globe in preparation for the next major disaster. In theory, these units could be delivered and assembled within a couple days after a natural disaster and be able to provide victims with a safe, secure, and durable shelter that could last from the initial emergency through transitional housing until permanent housing was constructed.

LEFT

Filling containers at the HabiHut Water Kiosk in Nairobi.

TOP RIGHT

Assembling a HabiHut Water Kiosk in Kenya.

ABOVE RIGHT

Another HabiHut in Nairobi.

PROJECT NAME
Life Cube
(http://www.lifecubeinc.com)

LOCATION
Santa Barbara, California, USA

PROJECT LEADER
Michael Conner

PROJECT CONSULTANTS
Patten Company
(http://www.pattencompany.com)

PROJECT YEAR
2010

PROJECT AREA
144 square feet

APPROXIMATE COST
$10,000

PHOTOS: Jamey Lantz (unless otherwise indicated)

Life Cube

Self-contained unit deploys in five minutes using inflatable technology and contains everything a family of four might need immediately after a disaster.

The ultimate in rapid emergency response would be a shelter that, at the push of a button, would unfurl into a strong, secure minihouse with all the tools and supplies a group of people might need stored inside. Certainly the technology for such a shelter is already available, so it was only a matter of time before someone integrated the disaster response strategies of rapid shelter and emergency supplies into one portable unit.

Michael Conner, a contractor and entrepreneur from Santa Barbara, California, was deeply affected by both Hurricane Katrina and the Kashmir earthquake in 2005. As he watched humanitarian relief efforts, he felt that a rapidly deployable, portable shelter could immediately help disaster-stricken areas, so he set out to create one. His aim was to design a shelter that was as

portable as a tent, as rugged as a trailer, and as rapid to deploy as an inflatable raft. The result of his endeavors was the Life Cube, a five-foot square box that can be moved to any location, unpacked, and set up in less than five minutes. Conner has worked closely with the Patten Company, the inventor of the inflatable raft, to design and fabricate the inflatable tent and airbeam technology (inflatable-structure support). Patten has helped ensure that the Life Cube is made from durable materials that are weather resistant, tear-proof, fire retardant, and exceed military specifications.

Everything that one might possibly need in the wake of an emergency is packed into the hard-sided black cube. Ideally, Conner hopes that someday these units may simply be airdropped

residents of the Life Cube will find a full supply of emergency gear, including a first-aid kit, a portable toilet, pots and pans, propane cooking stove, sleeping bags, air mattresses, water filter, buckets, flashlight, rope, duct tape, toilet paper, lighter, various tools, and a five-day supply of food rations for five people. An electrical package can also be supplied, which includes a battery, solar panel, inverter, lighting, AM/FM/CB radio, and an integrated fan in the roof for ventilation. Cargo nets can be hung from the airbeams to create storage areas. The Life Cube is intended to provide complete emergency assistance for up to five days until more help arrives.

where they are needed for the most immediate response, but until then, the 900-pound cubes will be shipped and trucked to the site. Upon arrival, units are doled out to those in need of shelter, who attach hoop rollers to the exterior of the cube and roll it to their selected site. The cube then unfolds and the hard sides of the shipping container become the sturdy foundation and floor of the shelter. After the tent is unfolded and laid out flat, the push of a button literally inflates the airbeams and the Life Cube takes shape. Tie-downs secure the tent to the foundation and only in heavy wind does the shelter need to be further staked out to maintain its rigidity.

The inflated shelter reveals a roomy, light-filled space with zipper windows, multiple doors, skylights, and a covered porch. Inside, the new

Life Cubes are meant to be reused, and Conner estimates the shelters are durable enough to withstand over fifty deployments, which certainly amortizes the high initial price. The shelters can be broken down and packed up in about half an hour for transport back to a warehouse facility to await the next deployment. Unlike any other emergency shelters, Life Cube comes automatically equipped with its own foundation and flooring, making it unique in the disaster-relief world. For situations in which supplies are not readily available, the Life Cube is a good option because it provides a full emergency-survival kit, as well as food, and can be set up very quickly. Though the shelter was primarily designed for

---

TOP LEFT

The sides of the cube are unfolded and set up to serve as the shelter's foundation.

ABOVE LEFT

Third generation of the Life Cube (left) alongside first generation (right) and one packed up inside travel crate (center). (Nick Pedersen)

TOP RIGHT

Life Cube moved on hoop rollers to the site.

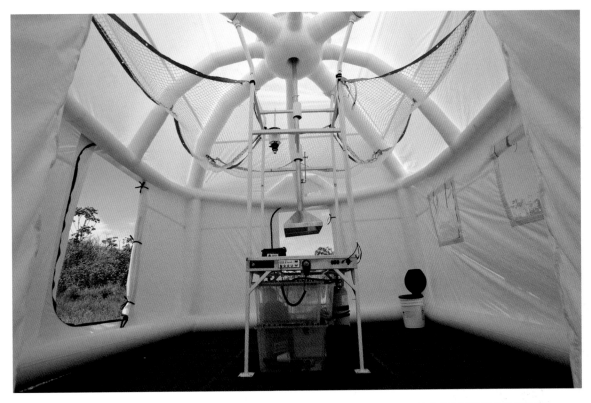

disaster and emergency response, it could also
be used for first-aid clinics, search and rescue
parties, and military command and control
stations.

The Florida-based Patten Company fabricates the
inflatable portion of the Life Cube, the rest of the
supplies are sourced in the Los Angeles area, and
everything is packaged together in Santa Barbara.
Since Conner first started working on his initial
design in 2005, the Life Cube has evolved into its
third generation and successfully demonstrated
its viability. In 2011 Life Cube sold one unit to
the Santa Barbara chapter of the Red Cross.
In the near term, the Life Cube will undergo
parachute-drop tests in order to optimize the
design for delivery via aircraft to quicken the
response time. Conner's ultimate goal is to
produce the best and fastest emergency response
shelter in the world. He hopes that one day his
organization will have the funds to be able to
respond to disasters on their own without
outside support or funding.

TOP

Interior view of the Life Cube.

ABOVE RIGHT

Central work table inside Life Cube. (Bill Able)

PROJECT NAME
Bamboo Shelters

LOCATION
Various

PROJECT TEAM
Gerard Minakawa of Bamboo DNA
(http://bamboodna.com) and Kevin
Rowell of The Natural Builders
(http://www.thenaturalbuilders.com)

PARTNER ORGANIZATIONS
Architecture for Humanity
(http://architectureforhumanity.org),
Kleiwerks International
(http://www.kleiwerks.com),
American Bamboo Society
(http://www.bamboo.org)

PROJECT YEAR
2008–2010

PROJECT AREA
80–200 square feet

APPROXIMATE COST
Undetermined

PHOTOS: Gerard Minawaka (unless otherwise indicated)

1.3

Bamboo Shelters

Renewable bamboo poles can be used to create fast, temporary shelters by weaving the bamboo splits together.

Rapid shelters need not be engineered, prefabricated, or delivered by a relief agency. In some instances the best way to provide quick, emergency shelter is to use materials that are on hand or harvested nearby. Lean-tos, tents, and huts can all easily be fashioned from a variety of materials, including branches, leaves, grass, found materials, tarps, fabric, and string. These simple shelters are enough to provide a roof over one's head and protection from the elements. Bamboo, recognized for its fast growing rate and strength for use in construction, is another material that can be used to build simple, fast shelters. This renewable material is found in various climates all over the world and can be harvested as needed or treated and stored for future use.

Bamboo builders Gerard Minakawa and Kevin Rowell have been experimenting and building with the renewable material for more than a decade. Together, they have completed some thirty large installations around the world for festivals and other events using bamboo poles and other simple implements. While traveling and building their installations, they use their downtime to experiment with bamboo splits, or sections of bamboo poles, to fashion quick shelters. Using nothing but the splits, string, fabric, and tarps, they have created dozens of small woven-bamboo structures. Like upside-down baskets, the shelters, made from natural materials, are sturdy, cost basically nothing, and leave no footprint behind.

Minakawa and Rowell source their bamboo from
various locations all over the world, depending
on where they are creating an installation. Sometimes they have to import bamboo; at other times
they can harvest it nearby. If the structure needs
to last longer than a year, they treat the harvested
bamboo poles by soaking them in a mixture of
borax and water. The borax helps to replace the
sugars in the bamboo, making it more resistant
to insects. But if the shelter is only temporary,
the bamboo does not need to be treated. Bamboo
poles can be used whole or cut into thin splits,
which are more flexible and easier to work with
than the entire pole. Bamboo splitters, machetes,
axes, table saws, and other power tools are used
to split the poles lengthwise into strips. After the
pole is split, a small blade is run along the sides to
remove any sharp edges.

To make a basic round bamboo shelter, strips of
equal length are used and a general footprint is
decided upon. Two strips are crossed in the center
and their ends are pushed into the ground as they
are bent downward to create the beginnings of a
dome. String, tied around the splits where they
cross, keeps the pieces from moving as more
splits are added to the structure. Like a basket,
bamboo splits can be woven to increase strength
and sturdiness until a basic domed shelter
emerges, leaving a space large enough for a person to crawl into. Tying more string around the
sections where the splits cross further improves
the structural stability, and rock anchors, tie-
downs, and stakes can help keep the shelter
rooted in place if conditions require it. After
the basic shelter is formed, tarps, fabric, plastic
sheeting, or other waterproof material can be tied
on to protect the interior from the elements.

Though Minakawa and Rowell have only been
using bamboo to create these rapid shelters,
other natural and available materials could
easily be used. Flexible branches, twigs, found

TOP
Woven bamboo shelter.

CENTER
The ends of the bamboo are stuck
into the ground to keep them in
place for short periods of time.

BOTTOM
The sturdy shelter can support
a person standing on top.
(visualfood.com)

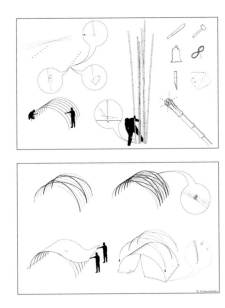

build these woven structures. In theory, these single-page guides could be distributed after a disaster with string and tarps so that victims could construct a shelter using bamboo or other available flexible materials.

Bamboo grows very quickly, becoming usable as a building material in a little over a year and full grown in five or six years, after which it begins to rot and decay. So using bamboo from sustainably managed forests is a very renewable practice. Bamboo is strong, lightweight, and, if treated and properly maintained, can last indefinitely, making it a viable building material for permanent construction. On the other hand, without treatment, bamboo makes an excellent material for temporary shelters that will eventually biodegrade and return to the earth. Minakawa and Rowell believe strongly in the usefulness of bamboo and will continue promoting the sustainable material and educating individuals on its use in the construction of both temporary shelters and permanent structures.

wood, strips of aluminum—basically any flexible material—could replace the bamboo strips to weave a domed shelter together. Grass, palm fronds, leaves, or other found cover material could be used if no tarps or plastic sheeting were available. The concept shows merely what is possible for anyone in need of emergency shelter. Even people lost in the backcountry could make use of these techniques to fashion a makeshift dome. The point is that available materials can be just as effective as manufactured parts to create rapid shelters.

Since their early experiments with the woven bamboo structures, both Minakawa and Rowell have led workshops to educate and train people in building simple structures with bamboo. Rowell led a bamboo-building workshop in Haiti after the earthquake and regularly teaches natural building courses through Kleiwerks International in North Carolina. In collaboration with the American Bamboo Association and Architecture for Humanity, Rowell has created a one-page illustrated manual showing how to

PROJECT NAME
Reaction Housing System
(http://www.reactionhousingsystem.com)

LOCATION
Austin, Texas, USA

PROJECT LEADER
Michael McDaniel

DESIGN TEAM
Frog Design
(http://www.frogdesign.com)

PROJECT YEAR
2011

PROJECT AREA
90 square feet

APPROXIMATE COST
$5,000

PHOTOS: Michael McDaniel

1.4

Reaction Housing System

Quickly transportable, stackable emergency housing system that sets up in a matter of minutes.

After Hurricane Katrina, Austin-based designer Michael McDaniel realized that America was woefully unequipped to provide emergency shelter after a disaster. As a designer at the very talented firm Frog Design, McDaniel knew he could come up with something better and cheaper than the travel trailers FEMA provided in the wake of the hurricane. McDaniel's design parameters were numerous: create a shelter that can be quickly deployed, easily assembled with no tools, big enough to house a lot of people, modular in design, reusable and finally, relatively inexpensive. So began his work to design the ultimate emergency shelter, as well as a sustainable system of emergency products that could provide immediate postdisaster aid.

The first iteration of his design sprang from the question of how to transport a ready-made shelter that would merely need to be set into place rather than assembled on site. Looking to other industries for inspiration, he came upon the coffee cup—stackable, insulated, sturdy, and easily transported. With the stackable shape of the coffee cup in mind, he developed the first prototype, which he built in his own backyard with locally sourced materials from vendors, friends, and hardware stores. This proof of concept, now known as the Exo-Alpha series, was built to test the size, connections, bunk-bed functionality, and mechanical systems. Once he demonstrated that his concept for the Reaction Housing System was viable, he, along with Frog Design, set about to refine the design, specify materials, and find a manufacturer that could produce the shelters.

OPPOSITE

Reaction Systems is currently working on the prototype of their Beta series of the Reaction Housing System.

35

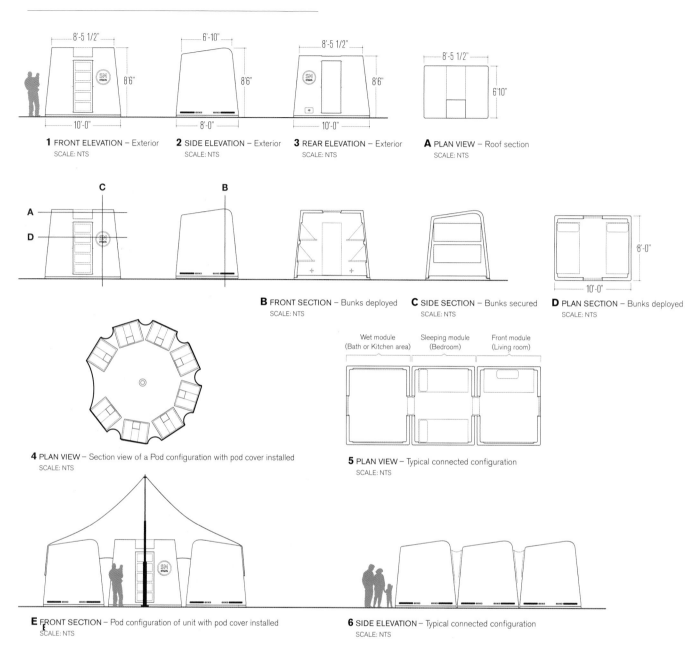

1 FRONT ELEVATION – Exterior
SCALE: NTS

2 SIDE ELEVATION – Exterior
SCALE: NTS

3 REAR ELEVATION – Exterior
SCALE: NTS

A PLAN VIEW – Roof section
SCALE: NTS

B FRONT SECTION – Bunks deployed
SCALE: NTS

C SIDE SECTION – Bunks secured
SCALE: NTS

D PLAN SECTION – Bunks deployed
SCALE: NTS

4 PLAN VIEW – Section view of a Pod configuration with pod cover installed
SCALE: NTS

Wet module (Bath or Kitchen area)   Sleeping module (Bedroom)   Front module (Living room)

5 PLAN VIEW – Typical connected configuration
SCALE: NTS

E FRONT SECTION – Pod configuration of unit with pod cover installed
SCALE: NTS

6 SIDE ELEVATION – Typical connected configuration
SCALE: NTS

7 SIDE ELEVATION – Shells stacked for transport
SCALE: NTS

8 SIDE ELEVATION – Floor plates stacked for transport
SCALE: NTS

ABOVE

Drawings of the Exo Unit.

The Exo is made up of two parts: a stackable shell that comes equipped with beds, outlets, and storage, and a base unit that the shell snaps into. The shell is made of a layer of foam insulation sandwiched between two sheets of durable plastic. The plastic sheets are made out of Tegris, a thermoplastic composite by Milliken & Company that consists of eighteen layers of recyclable plastic woven like a tarp and heat-pressed into a solid sheet, resulting in a material so strong that it has ballistic properties and NASCAR uses it in their cars. The load-bearing components of the shell are made from aluminum tubing. Each shell has a skylight and two doors and is outfitted with two sets of bunk beds built into the sides, two ladders to access the top bunks, lighting, and electrical outlets. Finally, the base plate is made from aluminum framing and composite decking material.

To transport the Reaction Housing System, the Exo unit shells are stacked on top of one another and loaded onto a flatbed truck along with the base plates. Measuring 9 x 10 feet, the units are easily transported by roadway without a special wide-load designation. One truck can transport 28 units, which can house 112 people. Upon arrival at the site, the base plates are unloaded by hand and set up in whatever configuration is desired, whether in rows, clusters, or a modular configuration joining multiple Exo units together. If necessary, sand or rocks can be dumped into the base plates to provide ballast against the wind. After the base plates are positioned, the 400-pound shells are unloaded and carried by four people, who set them on top of the base plates. Because the weight of the shell on the plate snaps it into place, no tools or skills are required to set up the shelter.

Stand-alone AC units or large HVAC systems and generators can be plugged into the back of the unit to provide power, heating, or cooling. Depending on the location, even distributed-generation solar panels or other renewable energy systems can be used as the power source. People

ABOVE

Inspiration for the emergency shelter came from a coffee cup, which provides insulation, is sturdy and stackable.

can move in immediately, unlatch the bunk beds, which fold down, and climb into bed. The insulated shell helps keep the interior comfortable and protected against both heat and cold, and the transparent doors and skylight in the roof help draw natural daylight into the interior.

Ideally, the Reaction Housing System would be stored in strategic locations around the United States and the world. As soon as a disaster happened, the shelters could be deployed and on their way to a safe location for setup. The units can be transported by truck, rail, cargo plane, or container ship. No tools or heavy machinery are required for setup, and the units can be carried by hand and moved if necessary. The Exo units can also be used for other purposes, such as toilets, showers, medical clinics, and offices, and connec-

tors can be used to bridge multiple units together to create larger spaces.

After the emergency is over, the shelters are easily hosed down and cleaned, then stacked up and transported back to the warehouse until they are needed again. The Exo unit has been designed for at least ten uses in its "lifetime," at which point, all of its components can be recycled.

At the time of this writing, the prototype has never been used in an emergency situation and the design is still being tested and refined. In May 2011, the Beta series of the Exo unit was built and demonstrated to various aid organizations in hopes of selling a large order to fund further research and development of the emergency shelter system. McDaniel would like to design a

full line of units and create a complete and flexible system that could address all aspects of the emergency. He would also like to develop a prefab house that would help during the transitional reconstruction period. Until then, the current Exo unit is flexible enough to be used as emergency housing and event space, and it even has military applications. Ultimately, McDaniel's goal for Reaction Systems is to have a sustainable business model that can fund innovation and make a significant and positive difference to disaster relief.

TOP LEFT
Rendering of Exo units arranged in a cluster by the side of the road.

ABOVE LEFT
Rendering of a single Beta Series Exo unit.

TOP RIGHT
Rendering of Exo units arranged in rows set up in a large parking lot.

PROJECT NAME
Recovery Huts
(http://www.recoveryhuts.com)

PROJECT TEAM
Harry Skinner

PROJECT AREA
100 square feet

LOCATION
Bellingham, Washington, USA

PROJECT YEAR
2006

APPROXIMATE COST
$1,200

1.5

Recovery Huts

Durable interlocking sections made of fiberglass form shelters that are quick to set up and could provide longer-term housing.

When the Kashmir earthquake struck in 2005, Harry Skinner was compelled to apply his forty years of architecture experience to designing a shelter that could do more than just protect victims of a natural disaster from the elements. His goal was to create a shelter that could be set up in less than an hour without tools and be sturdy enough to last until permanent housing could be rebuilt. After many design iterations, Skinner came up with a relatively simple concept— a series of hard-sided, identical, interlocking sections that snapped together. He named them Recovery Huts, anticipating that the shelters would be needed for far longer than temporary emergency relief.

In 2006, after hitting upon the right design elements for the shelter, Skinner launched his company. He settled on composite shell technology to create the sections, so that they would be durable, tough, and reusable. The shelters also have the potential to serve as homeless shelters, housing for search and rescue parties, temporary or worker housing, first-aid or triage clinics, and even storage units. Fiberglass construction allows the units to be reused many times, which would eventually offset their initial cost of $1,200.

Recovery Huts are composed of four equal sections that are eight feet tall with a radius of about five feet. Each section weighs sixty pounds, and the four sections can easily be maneuvered and assembled in less than half an hour by a single adult. Flanges on the edges of each section interlock with those on the neighboring sections and when set into place, they simply snap together.

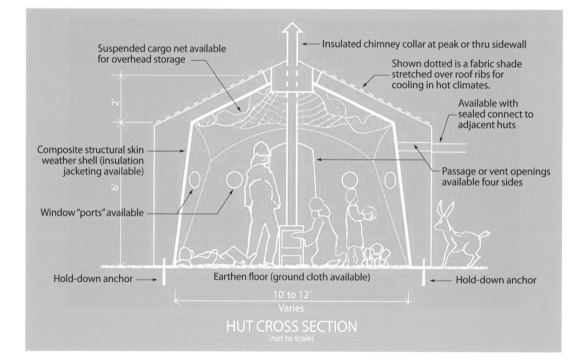

Suspended cargo net available for overhead storage

Insulated chimney collar at peak or thru sidewall

Shown dotted is a fabric shade stretched over roof ribs for cooling in hot climates.

Available with sealed connect to adjacent huts

2'

Composite structural skin weather shell (insulation jacketing available)

6'

Passage or vent openings available four sides

Window "ports" available

Hold-down anchor

Earthen floor (ground cloth available)

Hold-down anchor

10' to 12'
Varies

HUT CROSS SECTION
(not to scale)

TOP

Recovery Hut sections lying on ground.

ABOVE

Diagram of assembled Recovery Hut with solar fly shade device installed on roof.

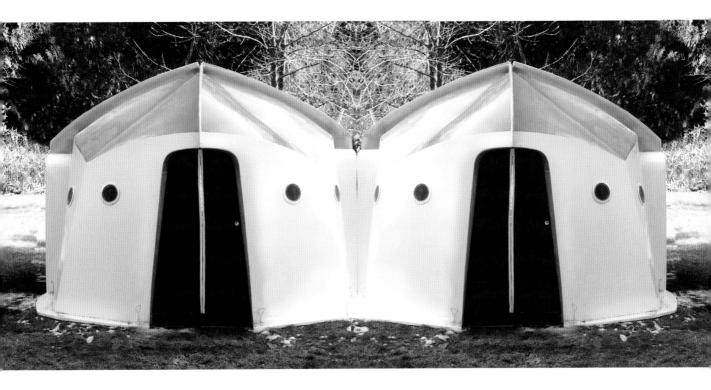

Once the sections snap together, the openings create two or four doors (depending on the design), allowing for multiple points of entry and cross ventilation. Five-foot-long channel caps fit over the flanges, and a top cap where the four sections meet makes the shelter waterproof. The top cap is held in place by a single bolt, which can be hand tightened, so tools are not necessary.

Tent stakes are driven through holes in the ground flanges to keep the shelter in place. Heavy-duty tent material with zippers down the center attach to the doorframes to protect the interior from weather or wildlife. Two porthole windows per section let in light and allow the inhabitants to see what is going on outside. Skinner has also designed a number of different accessories for the Recovery Huts to create a more comfortable living situation. There is a solarfly that can be installed on top of the shelter to shield it from the sun in hot climates. Conversely, a small heating stove and pipe, as well as insulated floor panels, can be added for warmth in cooler climates or seasons. Cooking and sleeping platforms, ground cloths, and hanging storage nets can also be added.

The fiberglass sections nest inside one another for storage and transport and could fit in a shipping container if necessary, but are best suited for transport via flatbed and truck. When the shipment arrives, individuals can simply carry their sections to their site and begin assembly without any tools. Recovery Huts can also be connected together to create multi-room setups that provide more space for a large family, a clinic, a command center, and so forth. For even more space, straight extender sections can be added to the normal four-section grouping.

ABOVE
Two Recovery Huts installed together
to form multi-room shelter.

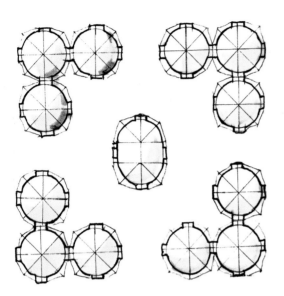
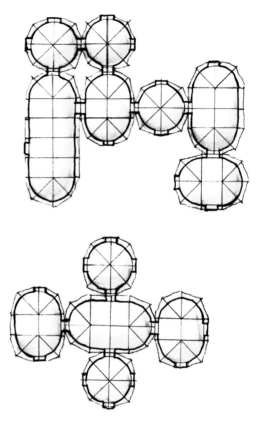

Hard-shelled shelters like the Recovery Hut have a number of advantages over tents and other rapid response emergency shelters. Recovery Huts are quite sturdy and were designed to withstand transport, inclement weather, repeated use, and harsh sunlight. If for some reason a section is damaged, it can easily be replaced, as all the sections are identical. Weight has been kept to a minimum so that an adult can quickly and easily maneuver the sections into place, and no tools are required for assembly of the shelter. The hut's low profile and hard shell allow it to withstand strong winds and storms. After the shelters are no longer needed, they can quickly be disassembled, pressure-washed, sanitized, if necessary, and nested together for transport to the next site. Although fiberglass is not generally considered to be very environmentally friendly, the sections can be shredded and recycled into other usable products at the end their lifecycle.

Currently, Recovery Huts are still in the prototype stage. Skinner has built two, but he hasn't had the chance to deploy them in a recovery situation. He continues to optimize the design, working to simplify the manufacturing and assembly processes, as well as to ensure the hut's comfort and security. Ideally, Skinner hopes to disseminate his design to organizations that will manufacture and store his shelters all over the world. If stored in key locations, Recovery Huts could quickly be deployed to whatever disaster or situation needs them.

ABOVE

Recovery Hut Village Layout Options.

TOP LEFT

Moving sections of the
Recovery Hut.

ABOVE LEFT

Placing sections of Recover
Hut into the right places.

TOP RIGHT

Assembling Recovery Hut.

ABOVE RIGHT

Exploded rendering of
Recovery Hut.

PROJECT NAME
ShelterBox Brazil Flooding
Deployment

LOCATION
São José do Vale do Rio Preto,
Rio de Janeiro, Brazil

PROJECT TEAM
ShelterBox
(http://www.shelterbox.org)

TENT MANUFACTURER
Vango (http://www.vango.co.uk)

PROJECT YEAR
2011

PROJECT AREA
approximately
100 square feet

APPROXIMATE COST
$1,000

PHOTOS: ShelterBox

1.6

ShelterBox

A British nonprofit organization packs boxes full of all necessary emergency supplies and deploys them quickly after disaster strikes.

In the twenty-four-hour period from January 11 to January 12, 2011, more rain fell in the mountainous state of Rio de Janeiro, Brazil, than is usually recorded in the entire month. The mountainous region became inundated with water, causing severe flooding and catastrophic landslides that killed hundreds in their paths. Many of the people in this region were poor and had built their homes on unsafe, steeply sloped terrain, which contributed considerably to the damage and loss of life. In total, 904 people perished from the floods and mudslides in the cities of Nova Friburgo, Teresópolis, Petrópolis, Sumidouro, and São José do Vale do Rio Preto.[1]

Responding to the tragedy, UK nonprofit Shelter-Box deployed their ShelterBox Response Team (SRT) to the region to assess the need for aid and

bring in their emergency response boxes to provide the initial supplies, including shelter, basic tools, cooking apparatuses, and water filters. The SRT estimated that more than 10,000 people had been displaced by the mudslides and were not able to return to their homes because these had been buried or severely damaged.

Former Royal Navy search and rescue diver and Rotarian Tom Henderson founded ShelterBox back in 2000. Its mission is to provide emergency shelter and warmth as quickly as possible without duplicating the efforts of other humanitarian aid organizations like the Red Cross. Henderson's organization originally started in the UK and delivered its first consignment of 143 boxes to earthquake victims in the Indian state of Gujarat in January 2001. The nonprofit now has

OPPOSITE
ShelterBox Camp in São José do Vale do Rio Preto, Rio de Janeiro, Brazil.

ABOVE
ShelterBox showing contents packed inside.

18 international affiliates and as of the beginning of 2011 had responded to some 140 disasters in over 70 countries, deploying more than 100,000 boxes.

In the case of the Brazilian mudslides, 107 boxes were delivered and set up in the town of São José do Vale do Rio Preto. The first responding SRT team was responsible for assessing the situation and finding a safe place to set up the shelters; a second team brought in and helped set up the boxes. Eventually 400 boxes in total were deployed, which helped around 4,000 people.

ShelterBoxes cost $1,000 each and are paid for through sponsorship by private donors and Rotary Clubs around the world. One unique aspect of the ShelterBox program is that donors can help fund a box or sponsor one by themselves. Upon ShelterBox's receipt of the funds, the donor is given a Box Number, with which he or she can track the box's location to see how and where it has made a difference. This approach helps donors feel directly connected to the victims and see how their funds are being used.

Operating out of the UK headquarters in Cornwall, the organization stockpiles all the necessary supplies for the boxes, packs them up and ships them out to strategic locations around the world for more efficient delivery when a disaster

strikes. Materials and items included in the 2.5 cubic-foot, rigid box are chosen for their long life, quality, and price, under the assumption that many of the items will need to be used for a year or more. The standard ShelterBox weighs about 110 pounds and includes the following items: a custom-made ten-person, all-weather tent by the UK firm Vango; a children's pack containing drawing pads, crayons, and pens; thermal blankets and insulated ground sheets for warmth; a water-purification device; a basic toolkit containing a hammer, axe, saw, trenching shovel, hoe head, pliers, and wire cutters; a wood stove or multifuel stove; and pans, utensils, bowls, mugs, and water-storage containers.

Sometimes other items like hats and gloves or school supplies are included, depending upon the severity of the disaster, location, climate, and availability of other supplies. In some instances, there are plenty of amenities available to victims except for shelter, so ShelterBox sends boxes packed only with tents. In other instances, the disaster wipes out everything, and victims are left with nothing, so additional items are included in the box. Over the years, ShelterBox has altered and improved upon the contents of the box in an effort to provide higher quality, more durable,

LEFT

Aftermath and damage due to flooding north of Rio de Janeiro, Brazil in February 2011.

RIGHT

Victims of flooding in front of ShelterBox tents in São José do Vale do Rio Preto, Rio de Janeiro, Brazil.

and more appropriate items for the given situation. The contents of the box are given to the families to keep. Sometimes they are passed on to other families in need, but they may be kept for use during the recovery and rebuilding process. In some situations in developing countries, the tents are the nicest accommodations families have ever had, and they continue to use them years after the disaster.

ShelterBox has become a successful organization in the last decade, responding to multiple disasters a year all over the world, including major events like the tsnuami in India, Sri Lanka, and Indonesia in 2005, Hurricane Katrina, the earthquakes in Kashmir, Haiti, and Chile, and the earthquake and tsunami in Japan, as well as smaller and more localized disasters like the mudslides in Brazil. The organization is often able to respond and deploy boxes within a matter of days, sending in their SRT on the day of the event to work with local authorities, the government, Rotarians, and other aid organizations in order to assess the need for aid.

The boxes are small and compact, making them easy to store and ship by whatever means, whether by boat, plane, camel, or even people carrying them. Though the box size is fixed, the supplies inside can be customized to the needs of victims and the price point of $1,000 each makes the whole package very cost effective. Their funding structure and box-tracking feature are effective tools for getting individuals to feel involved. Ultimately, their goal is to provide aid to half a million disaster survivors annually. As disasters continue to strike, especially in economically challenged and poorly built areas like the mountainous region of the state of Rio de Janeiro, ShelterBox will play a major role in emergency response and humanitarian aid.

NOTES

1   "Número de mortos na Região Serrana já passa de 900 após chuvas de janeiro" (Number of people killed in the mountainous region have surpassed 900 after rains in January). O Globo. Accessed 11 March 2011, http://oglobo. globo.com/rio/mat/2011/02/15/numero-de-mortos-na-regiao-serrana-ja-passa-de-900-apos-chuvas-de-janeiro-923809447.asp.

LEFT
ShelterBox Camp in São José do Vale do Rio Preto, Rio de Janeiro, Brazil.

RIGHT
Contents of the ShelterBox.

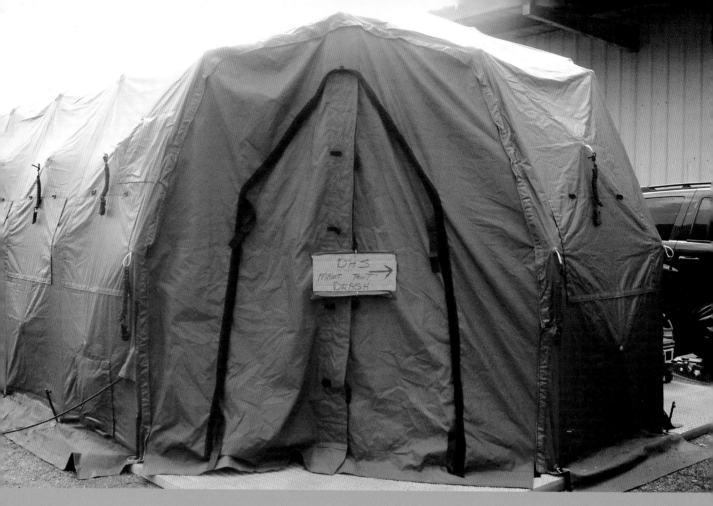

PROJECT NAME
Deployable Rapid Assembly
Shelter (DRASH)
(http://www.drash.com)

PROJECT TEAM
DHS Technologies LLC
(http://www.dhstechnologiesllc.com)

PROJECT AREA
748 square feet

LOCATION
Gulfport, Mississippi, USA

PROJECT YEAR
2005

APPROXIMATE COST
Undisclosed

1.7

DRASH Katrina

Military-grade shelters that are rapidly deployed for use in the field to assist emergency crews in recovery efforts.

Victims are not the only people who need shelter after a disaster. Military and relief teams and organizations respond to these emergencies and stay on site after the disaster to aid in the recovery efforts. These people also need adequate and safe living space in order to provide effective and immediate help. For emergency situations, medical, military, government, and civilian responders rely on rapidly deployable, soft-walled shelters and tents supplied by outside vendors. Often the shelter systems include command centers, kitchens, power generation, lighting, toilets, showers, and heating or cooling.

In the aftermath of Hurricane Katrina in 2005, one of the costliest and deadliest disasters in United States history, the National Guard,

among others, took part in relief efforts on the Mississippi coast . They were in need of housing and command and control centers, and DHS Technologies supplied both the National Guard and the Mississippi State Police with DRASH (Deployable Rapid Assembly Shelter) systems. After the storm made landfall in Louisiana and Mississippi and a needs assessment was conducted, authorities contacted DHS Technologies, who immediately responded with sleeping quarters, work shelters, hygiene systems, generators, and portable HVAC systems. For the next three months, emergency crews put the shelters to good use while they helped victims sift through the wreckage. Afterward, FEMA purchased the DRASH systems and placed them in their inventory for future disaster relief efforts.

Originally designed for military efforts, DRASH is a modern shelter system with a design based on the geodesic dome and constructed of an expandable, composite-metal frame covered in a durable, specially coated fabric. When packed away, the shelter is less than 2 percent of its fully deployed size. Only four to six people are needed to set up the shelter, a process that takes about fifteen minutes and requires no tools or special skills. The shelter is simply unpacked from its case and unfurled, and then the accordion frame is expanded and raised. The covering is already connected to the frame, so after the shelter is raised, it only needs to be anchored to the ground with tie-downs and stakes. Afterward, supplemental systems like lighting, HVAC, and power generators, which are transported on Utility Support Transport (UST) trailers, are connected to the tent.

Striking (taking down) the tent is equally quick and easy.

The unique, one-piece structural frame provides a clear, open-span interior space that requires no support poles to remain upright and rigid. Titanite®, an aerospace composite with structural properties 270 percent stronger than aluminum, is used for most of the shelter's frame. The shelter's covering is made from XYTEX®, a specially coated fabric that is fire retardant, mildew resistant, water repellent, and resistant to abrasion and ultraviolet rays. Designed for the harshest environments, DRASH is able to withstand heavy rains, high winds, extreme temperatures, and heavy snow loads. Durable and reusable, the shelters can be deployed repeatedly and are expected to last eight to ten years or more if properly maintained.

ABOVE

Debris from the hurricane litters the ground.

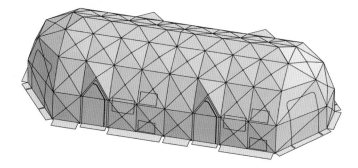

DHS Technologies supplies DRASH systems to a wide range of military and nonmilitary customers, but their primary customers are the U.S. Military, the National Guard, and NATO. Additionally, groups like the FBI, the Bureau of Alcohol, Tobacco, Firearms and Explosives, fire departments, police departments, medical examiners' offices, and public health departments rely on the portable, rapidly deployable shelters to provide shelter and command centers during investigations, emergencies, and search and rescue efforts. Aid organizations like the Red Cross have also purchased DRASH after emergencies to serve as headquarters in their relief efforts.

Manufacturing for the DRASH systems takes place in DHS Technologies' Orangeburg, New York, facilities. From there, the systems can be transported via commercial carrier or truck to their destination and then moved by utility vehicles to the site. For the Katrina deployment in Mississippi, DHS sent nine M Shelters, four 6XB shelters for female sleeping and working quarters, two hygiene systems with shower stalls and hot water heaters, a generator, and nine HVAC systems. Shelters can be positioned together and connected to create larger spaces, and the large, open-span space allows the tents to be used for whatever purposes may be necessary. A command center can easily become a hospital, triage unit, or even a school, depending on the situation and changing needs of the emergency.

In anticipation of future situations and threats, DHS constantly reevaluates their product line and develops new solutions to help first responders. Currently, DRASH is focusing their research and development efforts on technology that helps reduce the users' carbon footprint and maximize their capabilities in off-grid situations. They also have a new line of trailers equipped with Intelligent Power Technology™, which increases the life expectancy of the equipment and reduces fuel consumption by operating at optimum efficiency.

TOP LEFT
A row of cots inside the shelter.

ABOVE LEFT
Rendering of DRASH M Shelter.

TOP RIGHT
A row of portable toilets set up next to DRASH shelters.

PROJECT NAME
WheelLY

LOCATION
Rome, Italy

ARCHITECTS
ZO_loft Architecture & Design
(http://www.zo-loft.com)

PROJECT TEAM
Andrea Cingoli, Paolo Emilio
Bellisario, Francesca Fontana,
Cristian Cellini

COLLABORATORS
CISIA s.r.l. (Centro Ingegneria
servizi industriali Avanzati), Terni,
Italy (http://www.cisia.it); Logical
Art Effetti Speciali di Roberto
Papi, Papigno, Italy
(http://www.logicalart.it); Officine
F.lli Rosati s.n.c. Costruzioni
Meccaniche di Precisione, Terni,
Italy (http://www.fratellirosati.com)

SPECIAL THANKS
BOX 3 and Salvatore
Mauro and Anna Caré

PROJECT YEAR
2009

PROJECT AREA
38 square feet

APPROXIMATE COST
$1,040

PHOTOS: ZO-loft

1.8

WheelLY

A portable and expandable shelter provides storage and serves as a mobile home for the homeless.

Designing shelter for the homeless presents a number of challenges, as they are a unique subset with a dramatically different lifestyle from most. Homeless people tend to be nomadic, carrying their belongings in carts or on their backs, and they often collect recycling along the way to sell for money. Their lives require mobility, transportability, and security from those who might want to steal what they have. Many push shopping carts laden with their goods, while others carry bags or backpacks and may even have a tent and sleeping bag if they are lucky. Carts can carry a lot of things but offer no shelter, while tents provide shelter but are easily stolen. With all of these conflicting factors in mind, the Italian firm ZO_loft Architecture & Design set out to design a portable shelter for the homeless that solves the problems of mobility, transport, and shelter.

OPPOSITE
WheelLY Shelter in urban scene.

ABOVE RIGHT
Man pushing WheelLY through park showing advertisement on the side.

55

WheelLY is a rolling portable shelter in the shape of a wheel pushed by a handle, with two flexible tube tents that extend from either side. Inside, a hanging bag holds personal items or recycling as needed. The wheel, made of aluminum, is covered with rubber and rolls on a system of cylindrical bearings. It can be locked into place by pushing the handle down to the ground. One side of the wheel is covered with a neoprene disk that is attached to the polyester resin tent. When pulled out and set on the ground, the disk becomes an insulated ground cover for sleeping. The other side also has a pull-out tent but is open in order to access the interior or connect with other WheelLYs to create a larger space. Completely constructed out of recycled and recyclable materials, the shelter's impact on the environment is low and parts can easily be replaced if they wear out.

During the day, the user pushes his (or her) shelter as he goes about his business. At any time, the shelter can be locked into place vertically or can be turned on its side to become a seat. WheelLY can be used as a podium or seat to help the homeless in busking or performing in front of people or selling items like newspapers to earn money. At night the shelter is locked into place and the

TOP
Parked WheelLY with half of the tube tent extended.

RIGHT
Parked WheelLY with handle in locked position.

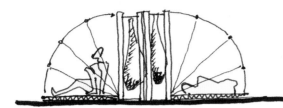

tents are pulled out and extended. The person sleeps on the side with the insulated neoprene disk and can use the other for their pet or for storage of personal items. In this way, the homeless person combines his shelter with his means of transportation and can keep his items secure when he is asleep. It would be hard for someone to steal the shelter or any belongings when a person is sleeping inside of it.

The estimated cost of the shelters is about $1,000, not terribly expensive but far more than a homeless person could ever afford. To solve the issue of cost, ZO_loft came up with the idea of using advertisements as a way to pay for the shelters. The neoprene disk on the side of the wheel doubles as a space for product placements.

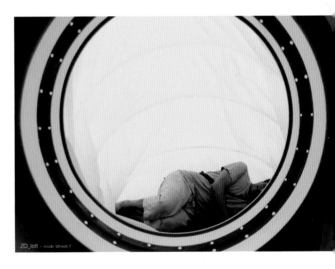

By paying to have their logo placed on the side of the shelter, companies could effectively pay for the cost of producing the shelter, thus offering them for free to the homeless. The shelters then become mobile billboards and an interesting urban dialogue.

The shelter was designed in 2005, while the ZO_ loft team was still in school studying architecture.

LEFT

Concept drawings for WheelLY and different ways the shelter can be used - Resting, Busking, Moving, Sleeping

RIGHT

Person sleeping inside WheelLY.

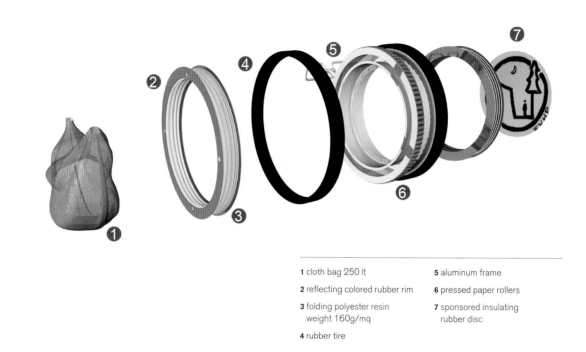

1 cloth bag 250 lt

2 reflecting colored rubber rim

3 folding polyester resin weight 160g/mq

4 rubber tire

5 aluminum frame

6 pressed paper rollers

7 sponsored insulating rubber disc

Since then, they have built and refined a prototype, which was shown around Italy in 2009. The team has also spent time with social workers and the homeless researching how the design might be improved, especially with regard to security, as robbery is a serious issue. Excited by all the positive responses the concept has received, they expect to produce five units for testing in Rome. Eventually, they hope a large corporation or government will purchase many units and donate

TOP

Exploded rendering of WheelLY.

ABOVE

Rendering of WheelLYs set up next to a store.

them to a social organization that will distribute the shelters for free. The team is currently looking for manufacturers and is continuing to refine the design and reduce the total weight to 30 kg (66 lbs).

Though some may be inclined to think we should not encourage homelessness with mobile shelters, the issue still stands that there are hundreds of thousands of people without a roof over their heads, and equipping them with a mobile shelter may be one of the best ways we can help them. WheelLY provides an interesting solution for homelessness that combines multiple needs into one compact and mobile unit. The solution also offers an enterprising way to pay for itself. In order to truly help the homeless, we must give them a way to help themselves, and this shelter could afford them the means to find stability and a source of income.

TOP
Parked WheelLY with handle in locked position showing advertisement on the side.

ABOVE
WheelLY fully extended in a park.

2.

TRANSITIONAL SHELTERS

A sturdy shelter that can help a family rebuild and expand as time and funds become available or a portable shelter that can be moved as needed.

In the wake of a disaster, transitional housing is often erected after the emergency period but before permanent housing can be built. It is a Band-Aid, a temporary solution that is not intended for long-term use. Like emergency shelters, many transitional shelters become permanent, either because it takes too long to build long-lasting housing or because funds never become available. Use of transitional shelters can be riddled with inefficiencies, require extra work, waste money and time, and even delay the permanent reconstruction process. On the other hand, there are times when a transitional shelter is absolutely necessary because a permanent solution is too far away.

A new wave of transitional shelters have been designed that can help families recover and rebuild in a more resource-efficient way. These shelters start off as a shell, but with some work, additional materials, and money, the shell can become a permanent home. Not only is this a cost-effective solution, but it involves the family in the reconstruction process, providing them with a sense of ownership and pride in their new home. A transitional shelter should be erected quickly out of high-quality and durable materials to ensure immediate protection from the elements. Then, over time, the residents can add on, build out, improve the conditions, and furnish the interior.

Another type of transitional shelter is the portable shelter, which can easily be transported for use in multiple places. Portable shelters may become more and more important as our climate changes, affecting food supplies, resources, and weather patterns, forcing people to accept a nomadic lifestyle and move frequently in order to find food and water. These portable shelters must be designed so that they can be packed up compactly for easy transportation, and set up quickly when the new location is found.

Whether the transitional shelter is meant to help in the reconstruction process after a natural disaster or in the transition to a new location, it must be flexible and adaptable. Design and use of transitional shelters should take into account the following elements:

1. **MATERIALS:** Ideally, materials are locally available and appropriate for use in the climate.

2. **COST:** Overall cost of the unit for manufacturing, delivery, construction, future improvements, and/or transportation should be kept as low as possible.

3. **CULTURAL ACCEPTANCE:** The design of the shelter should be applicable to the culture and appropriate for the climate.

4. **CONSTRUCTION:** Labor force, skill level, and material availability are major factors in the shelter's construction and should help support the local economy as much as possible.

5. **DURABILITY:** Design and construction should encourage permanence and be resistant to future disasters.

6. **IMPROVEMENTS:** The shelter should be relatively simple to improve in order to transform it into a permanent home.

This section looks at a variety of transitional shelters that make use of prefab elements as well as found elements to create the basic structure. Some can be transformed into permanent homes. The materials were chosen for their durability, longevity, and energy efficiency. A couple of portable shelters that can be easily packed up and moved if necessary are also explored. These mobile shelters have the ability to become permanent and improved upon if an ideal location is found. Transitional shelters are adaptable and flexible and can provide a low-cost yet sustainable solution for our changing world.

PROJECT NAME
Casa Elemental Tecnopanel

LOCATION
Constitución, Chile

ARCHITECT
Elemental
(http://www.elementalchile.cl)

BUILDING SYSTEMS
Tecnopanel
(http://www.tecnopanel.es)

DISTRIBUTOR
Sodimac (http://www.sodimac.cl)

ADDITIONAL RESOURCES
Sustainable Reconstruction
Plan for Constitución, or
PRES in Spanish
(http://www.presconstitucion.cl)

PROJECT YEAR
2010

PROJECT AREA
320 square feet

APPROXIMATE COST
$4,000

PHOTOS: Elemental

2.1

Casa Elemental Tecnopanel

Materials for an easily erected Structural Insulated Panel (SIP) home can be reused to build a more permanent home.

The earthquake off the coast of the Maule Region of Chile on February 27, 2010, rated 8.8 on the moment magnitude scale (MMS). Compared to the Haiti earthquake (7.0 MMS), which occurred a month and a half earlier, the Chile earthquake was 501 times stronger and initiated a tsunami that devastated several coastal towns. Luckily, however, the Chile earthquake caused fewer casualties overall. Chile has seen its fair share of earthquakes, including the strongest earthquake ever measured in 1960. Because of their history with seismic activity, the country was much better prepared than Haiti for a strong earthquake, in large part because of their strict building codes, but also because the epicenter was located offshore, whereas Haiti's earthquake originated right on the edge of Port-au-Prince. They were very different earthquakes with very

different results; nevertheless, more than 370,000 homes were damaged or destroyed and more than 500 people were killed in Chile.[1]

After the earthquake, the Santiago-based firm Elemental, which has considerable experience in social housing, was asked to help with the reconstruction plan for Constitución, the hardest-hit city. The Sustainable Reconstruction Plan (or PRES, which stands for Plan de Reconstrucción Sustentable) for Constitución is a master plan to rebuild the city in an energy-efficient, environmentally friendly, and sustainable way that creates jobs and promotes the quality of life. While Elemental was drawing up the master plan, they had the opportunity to help design and build transitional homes for a group of families. Their goal was to come up with an alternative

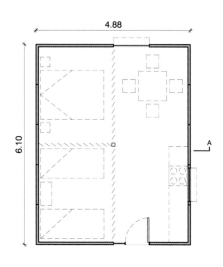

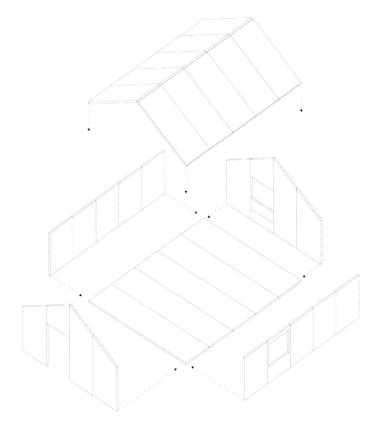

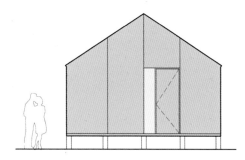

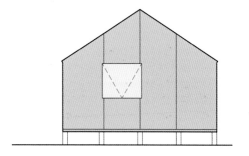

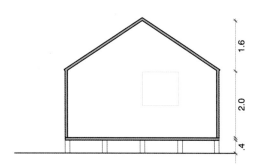

LEFT

Floorplan and side elevations of the Casa Elemental Tecnopanel.

ABOVE

Exploded view of the Casa Elemental Tecnopanel.

for housing in the aftermath of the earthquake that was not only quick to build but also allowed the homeowner to reuse the materials for more permanent construction.

The Chilean architecture firm teamed up with SIP maker Tecnopanel and distributor Sodimac to design and build the Casa Elemental Tecnopanel. Requiring fourteen SIPs, a few tools, and two days' work from three laborers, the house has a basic gable roof and large, open floor plan that is big enough for two bedrooms, a bathroom, a living room, and a kitchen. The fourteen panels are cut to create the different structural elements, leaving holes for the doors and windows. Every piece is utilized, so there is no waste in the process. The cut panels are easily connected together. A long ridge beam and a center vertical beam support the weight of the roof. The holes are filled with windows and a door that pull in natural daylight and encourage cross ventilation.

The SIPs serve as both structural members and insulation and require only simple exterior waterproofing such as tar paper or a coat of water-resistant paint. A simple pile or a concrete pier foundation is necessary for structural stability. Over time, the inhabitants could easily add on to or improve the structure, depending on their needs. Sturdier cladding and weatherproofing like corrugated metal or a moisture barrier would extend the life of the shelter, while interior amenities would make the home more comfortable. The structure could even be taken apart and the materials reused for more permanent construction if desired.

After building their first Casa Elemental Tecnopanel prototype, Elemental met and worked with a group of families to design a small camp in the city of Constitución. The firm donated their time and design expertise to build twenty private homes based on the prototype. In these more

ABOVE

Camp of 20 Casa Elemental Tecnopanel in the city of Constitución, Chile.

permanent renditions, a roof of corrugated metal was added and the exterior was coated with a waterproof paint. If these twenty home-owners want to rebuild in the future, they can easily dismantle the structure and use the parts and pieces again. A larger open-air structure of similar design, called Casa Abierto, was also constructed for community gatherings to discuss the city's reconstruction master plan and rebuild-ing efforts.

A number of years ago, Elemental developed a social housing typology that allowed home-owners to easily add to the basic design of their home. Versions of this type of adaptable housing for low-income families have since been built in Italy, Mexico, and Chile. The basic design is a three-story cinder-block row house with stairs leading up to an open deck on the second floor

TOP
Interior of Casa Tecnopanel.

ABOVE LEFT
SIP used to build the Casa Elemental Tecnopanel.

The basic principles of Casa Elemental Tecnopanel emerged from Elemental's work in social housing. The firm's goals for the transitional shelter were to make it easy to build, to maximize the use of materials, to include insulation, and to make it easy to reuse for other purposes. This simply designed home relies on minimal, durable, prefabricated materials that offer the inhabitants considerable flexibility as they transition from temporary to permanent housing.

and then into the home, which comes equipped with the necessary amenities. As a family grows and acquires funds, they can build rooms onto this deck space with whatever materials they have access to. The result is certainly eclectic, but often regionally and culturally appropriate, not to mention cost effective for those building the housing, as well as for the residents when it is time to expand.

NOTES

1   "Magnitude 8.8 - OFFSHORE BIO-BIO, CHILE"— U.S. Geological Survey. Accessed 9 March 2011, http://earthquake.usgs.gov/earthquakes/recenteqsww /Quakes/us2010tfan.php#

TOP

Families met with Elemental to discuss reconstruction in Casa Abierta.

ABOVE LEFT

"Casa Abierta" was built using the same techniques and materials as the Casa Elemental Tecnopanel and was used as meeting space during planning for the PRES (Reconstruction Plan).

PROJECT NAME
I-Beam Pallet House

LOCATION
Milan, Italy

PROJECT TEAM
I-Beam Design
(http://www.i-beamdesign.com)

**STRUCTURAL
ENGINEERING**
Gilsanz, Murray Steficek LLP

PROJECT YEAR
2010

PROJECT AREA
256 square feet
and up

APPROXIMATE COST
Undetermined

PHOTOS: Gabriel Neri, Suzan Wines, Samantha
Perry, Matthew Lloyd, Anzin Valy

2.2

I-Beam Pallet House

Shipping pallets, which otherwise end up in the landfill, become basic building blocks for a simple shelter that could transition into a permanent home.

I-Beam Design, a New York–based architecture firm, has been researching shelter designs for over a decade and hit upon what could be an ideal building block—shipping pallets. They are readily available, found all over the world, structurally stable, and most important, cheap. Each year approximately 150 million wooden shipping pallets are sent to the landfill in the U.S., but what most people don't realize is that these pallets can be used as building blocks for new homes.[1]

Azin Valy and Suzan Wines, founders of I-Beam Design, began working on shelter designs in the late 1990s and started working with pallets after Wines literally stumbled into a stack of them on her way home from work one night. Recognizing the simplicity and availability of the material, the duo began in earnest to formulate designs for pallet shelters. Further inspiration came from the fact that 84 percent of the world's refugees could be housed from a year's supply of American recycled pallets.[2] On top of that, pallets could be used to construct temporary shelters in a short amount of time, but owners could later modify their shelters with traditional building materials to transform them into more permanent homes.

Over the years, I-Beam Design has built pallet houses in New York; with architecture students in Indiana; in Milan, Italy, for the Architecture Triennale; and most recently in London, for Prince Charles's Royal Gardens, in conjunction with IBM, the Financial Times, and the Earth Awards. Built in 2010, this Pallet House used 100 pallets configured into floors, walls, and a roof for a 16 x 16 foot house.

OPPOSITE

Pallet House at Casa per Tutti Exhibition (May-September 2008) at the Architecture Triennale in Milan, Italy.

71

With modern tools and skilled workers, the Pallet House can be constructed in less than a week, but the shelter is also designed so that it can be built with only crowbars, nails, and hammers. Pallets are connected together on the inside with small cleats to create a wall assembly, which is then raised into position. The roof panels are assembled similarly, placed on top of the walls, and attached. Polycarbonate sheeting is then placed between the exterior and interior slats to provide a weather barrier for the inside but still let in daylight. Additional pallets can be used to create tables, benches, shelves, and even outdoor planters.

Pallets can be found just about everywhere, and most of the time companies are happy to give them away rather than figure out how to dispose of them or ship them back to their supplier. As a result, the basic building block for pallet houses is essentially free. The only other materials that are really necessary for the simple, temporary shelter are nails and polycarbonate sheeting, which are relatively inexpensive and easy to come by.

The beauty of the Pallet House, however, is that it can easily transition from temporary shelter to permanent house. Though the initial shelter plans are not designed for extreme weather or earthquakes, the shelter can be rebuilt on a sturdier foundation and shored up with studs to withstand strong winds and even seismic activity. It is also light enough to be affixed to a couple wheels and carted off to a new location. Then, materials indigenous to the region can be used to insulate and finish off the structure, making it not only more comfortable in the heat or cold but also more acceptable to the culture. Materials like wattle and daub, straw and plaster, foam insulation and plywood sheeting, or whatever is available and inexpensive could be used.

I-Beam's transitional Pallet House benefits from a number of design advantages that could make it a popular choice in the future, not only for disaster recovery but also for those building permanent homes. True, pallets may not be as readily available in the future, as companies reuse and repair more of their pallets rather than sending

them to the landfill, but for now, wooden pallets are widely available, easy to source, and often free to those who can cart them away. Only the basic of skills and tools are necessary to build a pallet house. The shelters can be upgraded in the vernacular style using local materials to create a permanent home that is adapted to the climate of the region. All of these factors contribute to making the Pallet House a highly sustainable building system capable of helping millions.

In the future, I-Beam hopes to expand the Pallet House project into a full-fledged organization that actively assists refugees and disaster victims worldwide. Ideally, I-Beam would like to align the project with pallet companies, suppliers, distributors, NGOs, and shipping companies to create a global system that can collect and deliver pallet shelter systems anywhere in the world. As the design now stands, a forty-foot shipping container can hold enough pallets and materials to build six shelters. If all of the pallets headed for the landfill in a year and a half were collected and utilized, there would be enough material to build housing for over thirty-three million refugees.[3]

NOTES

1 "Recycled Pallets Skid into U.S." Newspapers & Technology, September 1998. Accessed 2 February 2011, http://www.newsandtecharchives.com /issues/1998/07-98/pallets0798.html.

2 Humanitarian Projects, I-Beam Design. Accessed 2 February 2011, http://www.i-beamdesign. com/projects/refugee/refugee.html.

3 Ibid.

LEFT

Furniture can also be easily built from shipping pallets.

TOP RIGHT

The exterior of the Pallet House is simply covered in plastic polycarbonate sheeting and lets in ample daylight.

ABOVE RIGHT, LEFT TO RIGHT

Shipping pallet insulated with:
a mud and straw; **b** with styrofoam; **c** with rocks.

PROJECT NAME
SEED (http://seed-haiti.net)

LOCATION
Clemson University, Clemson,
South Carolina

PROJECT TEAM
Students of the Spring 2009
Architecture Design Studio at
Clemson: Adam Berry, Shannon
Calloway, Nick Christopher,
Maria Davis, Kristen Leanca,
Kyle Miller, Brian Miele, Sarah
Moore, Mitch Newbold,
Carson Nolan, Ayaka Tanabe,
Dustin White

PHOTOS: SEED

PROJECT LEADERS
Doug Hecker and Martha Skinner,
Assistant Professors Clemson
University School of Architecture
and cofounders of fieldoffice

COLLABORATORS
Bobby Weir and Tim Hayden,
Sargent Metal Fabricators

10^10 (http://10to10.org)
Welding: Paul Phelps, Tri-County
Technical College Department of
Welding

PROJECT YEAR
2009

PROJECT AREA
304 square feet

APPROXIMATE COST
Undetermined

2.3

SEED

Architecture and design students at Clemson University designed and built a prototype disaster-relief housing system for the Caribbean region out of an ISO (International Organization for Standardization) shipping container.

In spring 2009, students in an architecture and design studio course at Clemson University studied how ISO shipping containers could be used on a large scale in the Caribbean to provide recovery housing in the wake of a hurricane. Their research examined the movement of shipping containers in the region and determined that trade deficits left millions of empty containers in the ports. It is often too expensive for the shipping companies to transport the empty containers to places where they can be utilized, so they are just abandoned. Rather than leave them idle, the CU students, led by their teachers, Martha Skinner and Doug Hecker, proposed organizing a system that would utilize containers to create transitional homes, which could eventually be adapted into permanent housing.

They named the system SEED, an analogy for outfitting and delivering the containers and necessary supplies to families, who in turn would modify them and let them "grow" into homes. The containers are the seeds; they were chosen as the basic building block because of their great abundance and their physical characteristics. Without modification, a 40-foot shipping container can carry upward of 60,000 pounds and resist being overturned in 140 mph wind; it is thus incredibly strong and inherently hurricane and earthquake resistant. Moreover, ports have an entire infrastructure already dedicated to moving and repairing them. Finally, a 40 x 8 foot container makes an immediately available home of about 304 square feet. With time, modifications and additions can improve them,

turning the basic structure into the foundation of a permanent home.

More than just the modification of shipping containers for housing, the SEED system also includes essential tools for water and energy use. A water pod contains a basic composting toilet, rainwater collection system, and greywater recycling kit. An energy pod includes a basic cooking element, a small, thin-film solar panel, an electric outlet, and a battery. These pods could be prefabricated and stored in strategic port locations in case of disaster. To set the SEED recovery system in motion, the first step would be to deploy the SEED water and energy pods. Meanwhile, at the port closest to the disaster, modification of the containers would begin, which would include cutting windows and doors and installing any necessary hardware. At the same time, homeowners, cities, governments, and relief organizations would be working to clear rubble or damaged buildings from the disaster area.

Upon the arrival of the SEED pods at the port, each container would be outfitted with a water and energy pod, a canopy, a scissor foundation,

and a garden kit. Then the container would be loaded onto a truck and transported to the family's site. At first the container would serve as basic shelter, but as the family gradually built onto it, it would evolve into a permanent home, just like a seed that has been planted germinates, and finally grows.

During the 2009 spring semester, the students built a full-scale model of their shelter design on Clemson's campus to test out their theories. A container was shipped to campus and placed upon a stilt foundation with stairs leading down to the ground. Next, the walls were cut to create a foldout patio, a window with a raised shade,

---

TOP

SEED container houses create a new neighborhood.

ABOVE RIGHT

Rendering of SEED container house.

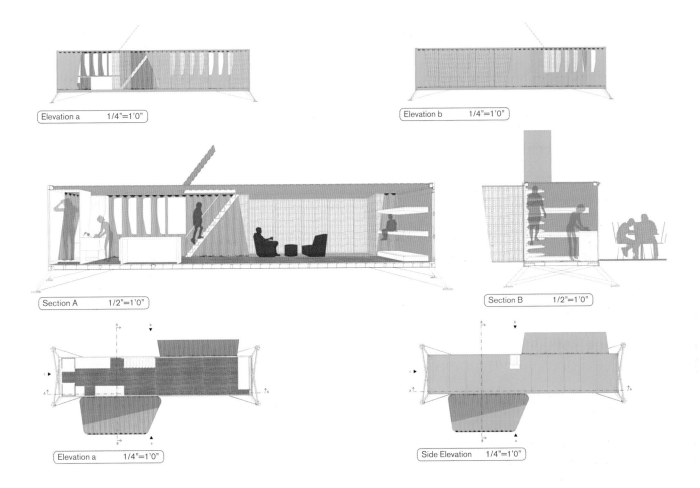

Elevation a   1/4"=1'0"

Elevation b   1/4"=1'0"

Section A   1/2"=1'0"

Section B   1/2"=1'0"

Elevation a   1/4"=1'0"

Side Elevation   1/4"=1'0"

and gill-like slits to encourage the flow of breezes through the container. Brightly colored paint brought the container to life, and basic plywood furniture made it more like a home. Without insulation, containers can heat up quickly in the sun, so the students installed a roof canopy made out of laser-cut steel; it not only provides shade but also allows air to move across the container to keep it cool.

The SEED prototype was designed for any country in the Caribbean, but less than a year later the project took on greater urgency. When the Haiti earthquake struck in 2010, Skinner and Hecker started receiving phone calls from humanitarian organizations all over the world in the hope that they had a workable solution that could be implemented quickly to help the Haitian people. Unfortunately, the student's research had only formulated the container-housing-pod system and built one prototype; in addition, many of the students had moved on and were working on new projects or had graduated. They had theories, but not a working model. As a result, Skinner and Hecker formed 10^10, a nonprofit design and architecture organization that has continued the students' research with the goal of turning the theory into a feasible and workable system.

ABOVE

Elevations and cross sections of SEED Haiti.

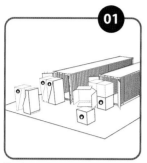

Hurricane A major hurricane makes landfall in the Caribbean causing billions of dollars in damages, killing hundreds of people, and leaving thousands homeless.

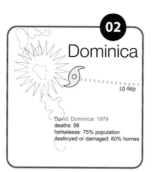

Hurricane A major hurricane makes landfall in the Caribbean causing billions of dollars in damages, killing hundreds of people, and leaving thousands homeless.

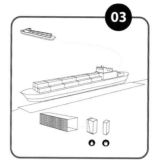

Dispersal 1 Following a hurricane, the seed packets are deployed via container vessels to the port where the need has arisen.

Modification Surplus containers are modified in port while the pods are in transit. Openings are cut into the containers in order to provide light and air and to expand the floorplan, providing maximum flexibility for future expansion and living arrangements. The port is the best location for this because in an emergency situation, it has the greatest concentration of resources (power, welding equipment, forklifts).

Debris Meanwhile, debris removal is occurring at home sites an on major roadways in order to facilitate transportation of the "seed" housing.

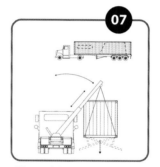

Fit out In the port, the elements of the emergency kit are fitted into the modified containers. Each container receives an energy pod, water pod, canopy, scissor foundation, and emergency garden.

Dispersal 2 The SEED home is loaded onto a truck and transported to the homeowner's cleared site.

Germination The container is placed on site with its deployable scissor foundation. The canopy and emergency garden are installed by the homeowners in their preferred configuration, and the family moves back in. The design's initial setting is an emergency shelter, but over time the shelter transforms into a permanent residence because of the adaptable nature of the design elements.

Currently, 10^10 is working on relief efforts to develop a 250-acre eco-village in the St. Michele region of Haiti as part of their SEED_Haiti project. Their current plan is to use shipping containers that are already in Port-au-Prince and the large number of shipping containers that are being sent to Haiti with relief supplies. Thousands of containers will soon be empty, and if they can convince the shipping industry to donate surplus containers rather than storing them or transporting them back, there will be plenty of containers to create houses. Though their research and work is geared toward recovery efforts in Haiti, whatever they create will be applicable to the entire Caribbean and maybe to the rest of the world. Additionally, work is under way for a SEED_Japan project to assist with reconstruction after the 2011 earthquake and tsunami.

ABOVE

Deployment process of SEED container homes after a natural disaster.

Seed packets The modifications to the container are designed to provide adequate ventilation, and open the container in such a way that the home eventually grows into the site with maximum flexibility. Additionally, all openings are designed so that the family's precious belongings can be loaded into the home and sealed up in the event of another emergency. The seed packets provide additional design elements that initially respond to the post emergency scenario, but eventually provide an improvement in the living standard of the occupants.

Emergency Garden The Emergency Garden is designed to get families back to a level of self-sufficiency in terms of food supply. The plants in the garden vary and are selected for growth rate and nutritional value as well as cultural appropriateness. The garden is shipped in sealed plastic 55-gallon drums with artificial soil and seeds in place. They are placed on the roof to receive sunlight and provide protection and to reduce heat gain on the spaces below and partially assist in storage of water for hygiene and drinking.

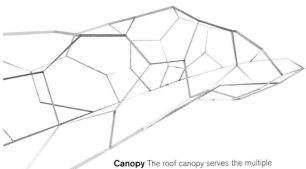

Canopy The roof canopy serves the multiple purposes of shading the container, capturing rain water for drinking, hygiene, and gardening, and providing additional space as a sleeping porch for larger families. The canopy is made of laser-cut spring steel sticks that can be configured differently for a variety of sites and homeowners. The design also has a repeated pattern of slots that maximize the flexibility of the home, allowing a variety of materials to be attached.

Water Pod The Water Pod plays a vital role in recovery by providing clean, safe drinking water as well as "off the grid" hygiene (a shower and composting toilet). Like the Energy Pod, the Water Pod is designed as a crate that functions both as packaging and as a semi-finished program element that the homeowner can finish over time with other materials (tile, plastic, etc.). The design is fully integrated with the Emergency Garden in that excess water is stored in the 55-gallon drums before being gravity fed into the shower. Potable water is filtered using an inexpensive multistep microbiological filter. Gray water exiting the shower is captured and used in the garden at grade.

Scissor Foundation The scissor foundation is attached below the container in the port. It is designed to unfold from below as the container is placed on site. The scissoring allows the foundation to be adjusted to varying topographies while the foot pads use low impact foundation technology that will work in most soils. The pipes driven through the pads create a structural wedge with the soil while resisting uplift in the case of a hurricane.

Energy Pod The Energy Pod is designed to the dimensional and structural specifications of a shipping crate. While in transit, it protects the contents and also acts as semi-finished packaging when installed in the container. It contains a 60-watt thin film solar panel to meet the basic needs of the homeowner for cooking, minimum lighting, and one electric outlet for power tools. When placed in the container, it also provides an initial space for storage, gathering, and cooking.

ABOVE

Accessories for SEED container homes.

PROJECT NAME
Groovyyurts
(http://www.groovyyurts.com)

LOCATION
Various, North America
and Mongolia

PROJECT LEADER
Yves Ballenegger

PROJECT YEAR
Since 2003

PROJECT AREA
130–530 square feet

APPROXIMATE COST
$4,850–$12,000,
depending on size

2.4

Groovyyurts

Yurts have existed for more than two millennia and are a portable, rapidly assembled, and energy-efficient housing solution with negligible environmental impact.

Traditional yurts have been around for more than two thousand years, have evolved to accommodate the lives of nomadic people, and are still in use all over Central Asia. In recent years, they have also become popular with North Americans and Europeans as recreational homes or additional living spaces. The round dwellings are easily heated, cooled, broken down for transport, and reassembled.

Traditional yurt makers throughout Central Asia rely on local woods for the frame, wool for the felt coverings, and horsehair ropes to bind the structure together. In Mongolia, yurts are intricately hand painted with beautiful, bright, Buddhist-inspired patterns, and much of the construction is rooted in symbolic numbers and tradition. In the West, yurts are constructed using more modern materials and are slightly taller, but the basic shape and design are largely the same.

Remarkably, since the days of Genghis Khan, who marched all over Asia in the early eleventh century with his troops wheeling their yurts behind them, only minor modifications have been made to the structure's design; it is truly a tried and tested housing solution. In fact, half of the Mongolian population, some 2.5 million people, still reside in yurts because of their nomadic lifestyle. Whether located on the windswept Central Asian steppes, in an alpine environment covered in snow, or at a state fair in the United States, yurts remain an exceptionally practical and sturdy shelter that can be erected in a matter of hours.

OPPOSITE

A yurt in the summer on a pier foundation.

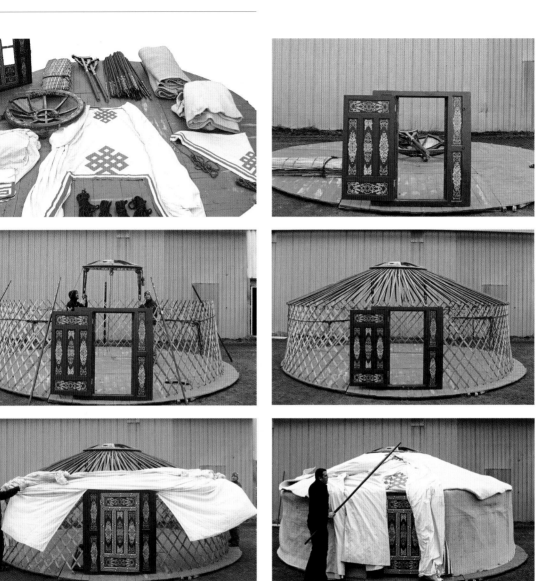

Yves Ballenegger imports traditional Mongolian yurts into North America, where they are often used as recreational houses or auxiliary dwelling units, like studios or guest houses. Ballenegger became interested in traditional yurts after a mission to Central Asia delivering school supplies through the organization Globetrucker. Rather than drive back to Europe with an empty truck, he bought four yurts and sold them upon his return. Ballenegger started his company, Groovyyurts, in 2003 as a way to help fund Globetrucker, but later split with them to keep the organizations' missions separate. Ballenegger buys directly from families who handcraft the yurts in the central Uvurkhangai province of Mongolia and take pride in

TOP LEFT TO RIGHT

Lay out all the parts of a traditional Mongolian yurt. Set up door.

CENTER LEFT TO RIGHT

Place roof ring on top of two central posts, the baganas. Finish laying roof beams.

BOTTOM LEFT TO RIGHT

Begin covering structure with first layer of cloth. Spread out water resistant canvas cover.

the fact that no nails are required for construction. Groovyyurts is one of many companies that either import or manufacture yurts in the West, but it serves as an excellent example of the traditional Mongolian yurt.

Groovyyurts are composed of a series of expandable wood lattice sections, called khanas, that are placed together to form the round exterior. The greater the number of lattice sections, the larger the diameter, which can range from eight to forty feet. A roof ring, called the toono, is the most important element of the yurt and is positioned at the center of the yurt on top of two central posts, the baganas. Then eighty-one rafters are placed between the wall and the toono to form the roof. When the basic structure is completed, it is covered with large sheets of felt, which

provide insulation. The felt is topped with a layer of water-resistant canvas and a final decorative white cloth. All the coverings are held in place with horsehair ropes. At around eight hundred pounds each, the yurts can be transported via ox, yak, pulled cart, or on the backs of two camels. An experienced family can assemble their home in less than an hour.

The roof rafters, roof ring, and furniture are constructed from locally sourced aspen, pine, or birch and are hand painted with beautiful patterns. The thick layers of felt provide enough insulation to keep the inhabitants warm in below-freezing temperatures during the winter. In the summer, the white coverings reflect the hot summer sun, and the covers are raised up from the bottom to encourage natural ventila-

TOP LEFT	TOP RIGHT	ABOVE
Continue spreading out exterior cloth cover.	Wrap yurt in rope to hold cloth in place.	Yurts in a landscape.

tion. In the late eighteenth century, stoves and stovepipes were introduced in Mongolia, an amenity that vastly improved the comfort of yurt dwellers, who previously had to cope with the smoke from the fires they lit inside the shelter. Because of their low profile, yurts are extremely sturdy and can withstand heavy winds and snowfall. To minimize their impact on the land and to respect the earth, yurts are not typically staked down, but if the wind is strong, the shelter is held in place by attaching the roof ring to a heavy rock placed inside the yurt.

Modern and Western yurts retain some of the traditional elements of the original yurt, including the expandable lattice frame, but make use of modern materials like vinyl for the exterior covering. Vinyl is more weather resistant and durable but less breathable than organic materi-

als like felt. Westerners have also increased the height of yurts to accommodate a taller stature and have added skylights, windows, and more modern amenities. The Western yurt is generally lower-maintenance than traditional yurts, which often need adjustments, but the Western yurt is not as easily heated or cooled as its Mongolian counterpart. In developed countries, yurts are transported by car or trailer, depending on their size, and can also be quickly assembled.

For a long time, yurts have proved to be an excellent shelter for people who move often to take advantage of different locations and seasons. They are easily transported, quickly assembled and disassembled, and comfortable in hot and cold weather. Their low, sturdy profile allows the wind to flow over and around them, enabling them to withstand the harshest of climates and

conditions. The traditional nomadic cultures of Central Asia rely on their environment for everything, and the yurt provides them with a close connection to nature. In the West, too, those who live in yurts are often looking for a closer connection with, and a way of reducing their impact on the environment.

Yurts have been a tried and tested solution for rapid and portable housing. They are also sturdy and can last indefinitely, if taken care of properly. As the climate changes and becomes more extreme, certain groups of people around the world may be forced to move with the seasons, and a yurt is an excellent option for a nomadic lifestyle.

TOP

A yurt in snow.

ABOVE LEFT

Interior of a yurt with handmade traditional furnishings.

PROJECT NAME
Steel Elements Shelter

LOCATION
Port-au-Prince, Haiti

PROJECT TEAM
Steel Elements International
(http://www.steelelements.com)

PARTNER ORGANIZATIONS
CHF International
(http://www.chfinternational.org)
and USAID (http://www.usaid.gov)

ADDITIONAL RESOURCES
Emergency Housing for Haiti
(http://www.ncyhousingforhaiti.
com)

PROJECT YEAR
2010

PROJECT AREA
200 square feet

APPROXIMATE COST
$1,200

PHOTOS: Steel Elements International LLC & S.A.

2.5

Steel Elements Shelter

Steel-framed housing kits provide sturdy starter homes that protect Haitians from the elements and can later transition into permanent homes.

Shortly after the Haiti earthquake in 2010, Scott Coulombe, CEO of Steel Elements International, received a phone call about a new idea for temporary housing. The caller had built a basic shelter out of bamboo, but thought it could be even better if made out of steel. The steel manufacturer had considerable experience with framing systems for large buildings, schools, hotels, and more, but he had not yet moved into the field of humanitarian design. With the concept in hand, Steel Elements rapidly developed and designed a building kit for a basic one-story, 10 x 20 foot home.

By early spring 2010, Steel Elements was working with CHF International and USAID to ship thousands of shelters to Haiti as quickly as possible. The kits were manufactured at the

Steel Elements factories in New Hampshire and Florida and then packed into shipping containers for transport to Haiti. The steel members are C-shaped and nest inside one another, which enables the company to pack enough materials in a 20-foot container to build 50 shelters. Adhering to the minimum standards of 38 square feet per person set by Sphere, each shelter can house up to 5 people, so one full shipping container can provide shelter for 250 people.[1]

The basic shelter is composed of durable cold-formed, light-gauge steel members cut to specific lengths that are joined together with screws and topped off with a galvanized-metal roof. Easily assembled with few tools and unskilled labor, the basic shelter can be put up in about a day's time. Initially, the shelters are wrapped in plastic sheet-

---

OPPOSITE

A group of shelters set amongst walls under construction.

ABOVE

Until more permanent materials can be acquired, the shelters are covered in a weatherproof plastic sheeting.

ing or tarps for privacy and additional protection from the elements. Over time, however, residents can add more permanent features like exterior walls and interior amenities to the strong steel frame.

Each pre-cut structural member and part is numbered to expedite assembly as soon as the containers reach their destination. In Léogâne, a town west of Port-au-Prince that was at the epicenter of the earthquake, a team of unskilled local workers was hired to construct these "kit homes." Despite difficult building conditions, rubble everywhere, and unreliable power, the local and humanitarian aid workers prevailed and quickly learned how to assemble the parts into a sturdy shelter. The screws are coated to prevent rusting and the steel roofing material is coated with Galvalume to reflect the sun's radiant energy and prevent overheating. The shelters were wrapped in sheeting and anchored into the ground with earth screws or foundation anchors, but they could easily be moved onto a sturdier foundation of concrete piers or a concrete slab.

LEFT
Assembled Steel Elements shelters in Haiti.

TOP RIGHT
Materials for Steel Elements shelters, stockpiled and waiting for assembly.

CENTER RIGHT
Training workshop to teach laborers in Haiti how to build the shelter.

ABOVE
Workers moving a prefabricated wall assembly.

Shelters are given to those whose need is greatest—the people whose homes were completely destroyed, who lost wage earners, or who have disabled family members. Over time, families can make their shelters more permanent by adding interior walls and exterior cladding, which can be just about any kind of material they can find or afford. By finishing the shelter with durable materials, it could easily last for a hundred years, far longer than a wood-framed or masonry home. The structural steel frame ensures that the homes can withstand earthquakes, hurricanes, fires, pests, and mold, and it is even moisture and corrosion resistant.

The steel shelter has many advantages over similar wooden shelters that have been built nearby in Haiti. Manufacturing and shipping are easy and economical because the materials can nest, enabling many units to be shipped in a small space. Steel Elements makes use of high-content recycled steel for the members, which can be recycled again at the end of the building's life. Two men can assemble the shelters in one day following the step-by-step illustrations supplied with the kits. If need be, the steel frame can be picked up and moved to another or a more suitable location with ease. The best part of the steel-frame shelter system, though, is its ability to transition into a permanent home using whatever materials are culturally acceptable, economical, and most important, available.

By the start of 2011, over 3,500 steel shelter kits had been delivered and assembled in Port-au-Prince, Tabarre, Nazon, Petionville, Léogâne, Carrefour, Gressier, Petit Goâve, Grand Goâve, Les Cayes, and Croix-des-Bouquets. Steel Element's goal was to ship another 6,000 shelters by the end of 2011, providing shelter for 30,000 more people. The company is now working on new models with more amenities and features, geared toward middle-class families, as well as a larger two-story home. They are also developing plans for steel-frame schools and culturally acceptable housing to replace poorly built slums around the world, especially in places like Brazil and India.

NOTES

1   The Sphere Project: Humanitarian Charter and Minimum Standards in Humanitarian Response (http://www.sphereproject.org)

LEFT

Interior of an assembled Steel Elements shelter.

RIGHT

A fully completed Steel Elements shelter with a plaster façade and louvered windows.

PROJECT NAME
Uber Shelter
(http://www.ubershelter.org)

LOCATION
Port-au-Prince, Haiti

PROJECT TEAM
Rafael Smith, Armand Mulin,
Bob Proctor, Brad Milius,
Josh Messmer, Arthur Smith,
Mercedes Plant, Chayzee Allen,
Richard Gustafson, Desmond Tardy,
Steven Elias, Bruce LeBel,
Phanor Mendelking

PARTNER ORGANIZATIONS
Unreasonable Institute, Accelerating
Possibilities, World Shelters, NW Packaging

PROJECT YEAR
2011

PROJECT AREA
250 square feet

APPROXIMATE COST
$3,200

PHOTOS: Laurel Cummings (unless otherwise indicated)

2.6

Uber Shelter

A flat-packed metal and plastic shelter shipped to the site of an emergency provides immediate housing that could transition into a more permanent structure.

Rafael Smith saw a gap in the market for shelters following disasters, so for his undergraduate thesis in industrial design, he worked on a concept for a transitional shelter that could immediately help victims and eventually transition into permanent housing. After winning a number of design awards and some funding, Smith built a prototype, and by the time the earthquake in Haiti struck, his design had evolved into the Uber Shelter and was ready for field testing. More than your basic emergency shelter, the Uber Shelter is a housing system that can assist in emergency relief efforts, transition into sturdier, temporary housing, and eventually be modified into permanent housing.

When Smith was designing the shelter, he focused on six key factors as guidelines. First, the shelter

needed to be easily transported, shipped flat, carried by hand, and of a size that fit into a pickup truck. Second, it needed to be easily assembled without the use of power tools. Third, it needed to be raised off the ground in the event of heavy rain and flooding, and have the ability to be built on uneven ground. Fourth, it needed to have a small footprint, as land is scarce after a disaster and a small footprint maximizes land use for all. Fifth, it needed to be entirely reusable and have the ability to be moved to another location. And sixth, it needed to be adaptable to local conditions and materials, and be able to grow as needed.

The resulting design for the Uber Shelter is a prefabricated, flat-packed, easily assembled, two-story modular shelter built on telescoping

OPPOSITE

Uber Shelter is a prototype for a transitional shelter that can help families after an emergency.

ABOVE

Elevation of the Uber Shelter.
(Uber Shelter)

91

legs. The frame is constructed out of roll-formed steel with plywood flooring, and the walls and roof are corrugated polypropylene sheets. All of the materials pack tightly into three 400-pound packages that can be carried by six people and loaded into the back of a pickup truck. All three packages fit in a 4 x 8 x 2 foot space. When the packages arrive on site, the parts are unpacked and the frame and floors are assembled using only a wrench, ratchet, and screwdriver. Next, the bracing and wall supports are installed, then the walls and roof supports, the doors and windows, and finally the roof. A sleeping loft and living space are located on the second floor and the kitchen is situated on the lower floor. A shaded porch provides covered space for various activities; it can be enclosed for additional interior space.

After a disaster, the Uber Shelter could be delivered in parts to provide different stages of housing. First, for immediate relief, the frame and flooring would be delivered to the victims, who would use plastic sheeting for the walls, creating the most basic of shelters. A second shipment would then be delivered, including the walls, windows, doors, and roofing. Eventually, shipments of additional modules could be delivered to expand the units into different configurations. Realistically though, the residents would source local materials to outfit their shelter over time, making it stronger and more permanent. Smith's ultimate goal is not for these shelters to be handouts, but to be catalysts for development. While the basic frame might be prefabricated elsewhere and delivered to the place of disaster, the other necessary parts could ideally be manufactured nearby, providing the local people with jobs and making use of local and culturally acceptable materials.

In early 2011, Smith and his team traveled to Haiti with two hand-built prototypes to test the

TOP

The two-story Uber Shelter provides more secure housing after an emergency.

ABOVE

Uber Shelter is packed up and ready for transport to Haiti.

design in the field. Two families received the shelters and reported their experiences to Smith, whether positive or negative. One of the shelters went to a community leader named Genesis and his family, who live in Delma 33 Adoken, an IDP (internally displaced person) camp in Port-au-Prince with over 30,000 residents living under tarps and stick frames. Genesis and his enterprising family are working to make the community safer and have started a beauty salon as well as a cyber café under a tarp. The other recipient of an Uber Shelter is a woman who lived in a camp in Port-au-Prince but wanted to move out, because she felt so unsafe. Her sister owns land outside the city center and has let the woman, her child, and her mother set up the shelter there.

Smith and his team will take what they learn from both families' feedback to improve upon the design of the shelter. They also hope to have more in-depth conversations with aid organizations to understand the best methods for delivery and implementation of shelter projects after disasters. Smith has spoken with several manufacturers to create a product that can be partially or fully manufactured in a field production site in the disaster area to maximize work opportunities for those affected by a disaster. Smith would also like to build a pop-up school based on the Uber Shelter technology in order to help communities and children get back to their normal lives more quickly.

TOP LEFT

Rendering of Uber Shelter with side walls removed to see inside. (Uber Shelter)

TOP RIGHT

Rendering of Uber Shelter as side walls and windows are installed. (Uber Shelter)

BOTTOM LEFT AND RIGHT

Assembly of Uber Shelter in Haiti.

PROJECT NAME
AirClad Roofpod
(http://www.airclad.com)

PROJECT TEAM
AirClad by Inflate

PROJECT AREA
485 square feet

LOCATION
London Fields, London, UK

PROJECT YEAR
2010

APPROXIMATE COST
$20,474 (£13,050)

PHOTOS: Jason Toser (unless otherwise indicated)

2.7

AirClad Roofpod

Inflatable and portable architecture merge to create a podlike and efficient structure suitable for temporary and semipermanent use.

Homes and shelters of the future are likely to move beyond traditional building materials like timber, concrete, and glass. One enticing option could well be air, a natural insulator and mostly free, so it stands to reason that it might make good, inexpensive walls if you could harness it. One way to harness air is to trap it inside an impermeable membrane, similar to a balloon, and inflate the material to create a semisolid surface. Many such inflatable structures have been built around the world and are often used for temporary events.

Nick Crosbie, a British designer, started designing inflatable products when he was in college in London, and over time his work evolved into building inflatable structures used primarily for marketing and events. The structures were

dynamic, graphic, and temporary, and packed down to a small size, which made them excellent for travel. Crosbie's company, Inflate Products Ltd, emerged out of this early work, and since the late 1990s, the firm has produced hundreds of temporary inflatable structures. These structures function like outdoor tents and event spaces, which are pressurized to stay afloat and tethered down to stay in place. Inflate has customized temporary structures in the shapes of domes, cubes, and shells for the likes of Virgin Galactic, Motorola, Absolut, Boeing, Ford, Puma, and Red Bull.

In 2008, Crosbie began working on a new product—a lightweight structure that felt more permanent than his regular inflatable event spaces. Crosbie wanted to expand his

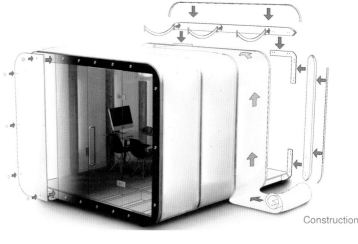

Construction

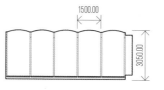

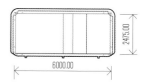

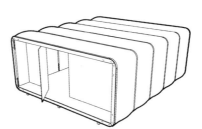

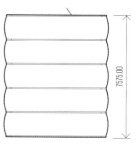

AIRpod 6x7.5m

line to reach customers who were looking for extra living space, rooftop offices, or temporary shops that needed more secure foundations, walls, and amenities. In 2009, Inflate unveiled the AirClad, a semipermanent-to-permanent structure composed of a skeletal frame covered in an inflatable skin atop a solid foundation. The structure is sturdy and durable enough to withstand inclement weather, and with its straight walls the interior can be outfitted and decorated. Up to 20 meters long and six meters wide in one-meter increments, it can be customized to suit customers' specific needs, making it perfect for retail shops, hotel rooms, backyard or rooftop offices, studios, apartments, or extra living spaces. AirClads are built in the UK, arrive flat packed, assemble in a matter of days, and can always be dismantled, packed up, and moved again.

The wood joists of AirClad's skeletonlike frame are made from spruce plywood sourced from Finland; they are CNC (computer numerical control) cut and connected together with steel joints and bolts. Cut lumber is fitted between the frame elements to form the floor platform, and curved wall and ceiling joists hold the frame in place. Plywood sheets are laid to create the floor, walls, and ceiling. After the main structure is in place, aluminum rails are installed on the timber joists, and the inflatable cladding is stretched on. The choice of cladding material depends on the performance needs of the building, but it is typically ETFE, silicon glass, or PVC. Once the cladding material has been put on, tubing is inserted into each cavity and the pillows are inflated until they are stretched taut. Some air loss is to be expected over time, so an air blower provides extra pressure as

needed. Finally, a glass seal with an integrated door caps each end of the structure.

The cladding material provides a watertight seal over the entire structure, has its own natural insulative properties, and reduces solar heat gain. Mechanical AC and heating units can be added as needed, and under-floor heating elements work especially well with the design. Lighting, built-in furniture, and other amenities can be added upon request. Since most of the structure by volume is air, it is quite lightweight and requires a minimal foundation of concrete footings if intended as a permanent structure. If the AirClad is only temporary, there may be no need for a foundation at all.

Fabrication of the parts for the shelter produces very little waste, unlike traditional stick-built homes. Transportation of the AirClad is simple and efficient, as all materials can be flat packed and shipped to the site. Generally, a 10 x 10 meter (100 square meter) AirClad will fit into a 4 x 1 x 1 meter space on a pallet, which is easily transported by truck, inside a container, or by rail.

Depending on the size of the structure, assembly takes two to four days and disassembly takes a similar amount of time. These reusable structures can be put together, taken apart, and transported to any number of locations, making them an interesting option for transitional shelters. They could even be expanded, either by adding more AirClads or by building other structures alongside them. If parts ever break or wear out, the modular design makes part replacement easy.

As of early 2011, AirClad had built five of these structures, three of which have become permanent. Inflate owns one of the structures, which serves as extra office space on the roof of their factory in London Fields. With their light footprint, AirClads offer a natural solution to the need for additional living space in crowded urban areas. The modular parts could literally be walked up the stairs and assembled on just about any rooftop. Though radical and untraditional, AirClad is a unique housing typology that can fit in practically any location and provide temporary or even permanent shelter.

ABOVE

AirClad Roofpod on top of Inflate's headquarters in London.

PROJECT NAME
Shelter 2.0
(http://www.shelter20.com)

CNC CONSULTING
Bill Young, Shop Bot
(http://www.shopbottools.com)

PROJECT AREA
140 square feet

LOCATION
Atlanta, Georgia, USA

WEB SITE DEVELOPMENT
Becky Shumacher

ADDITIONAL RESOURCES
Mad Housers
(http://www.madhousers.org)

PROJECT LEADER
Robert Bridges

PROJECT YEAR
2010

APPROXIMATE COST
$2,900

PHOTOS: Shelter 2.0

2.8

Shelter 2.0

A computer-cut, flat-packed shelter design is offered free through an open-source license in order to provide housing for disaster victims and the homeless.

Robert Bridges was first inspired to build a shelter after working on a barrel-vaulted ceiling in a home he was helping construct. He thought that the stable, arched roof design could make for a very strong shelter and that by using a computer to digitally fabricate the parts, he could easily build housing for the homeless around the world. With his background in construction and carpentry and his skills with computer-aided fabrication, Bridges set out in 2009 to design an arched-roof shelter out of oriented strand board (OSB) cut with a computer numerical control (CNC) machine. A year later, after a couple of design evolutions and entries into various design competitions, Bridges had a working model, which he built to serve as a tent during a local Relay For Life race in eastern Virginia.

This first incarnation, the Exmore Shelter, was a 10 x 16 foot structure made out of puzzlelike parts cut by a CNC machine. Digital cutting machines allow for very precise cuts and parts that are exactly the same every time. Bridges first created a computer model of the shelter, then broke it down into the individual parts to create a template that the machine uses to make the cuts. After all the parts are cut, the shelter can be flat packed for delivery in a space less than 4 x 8 feet. Enough material for twenty shelters can fit inside a twenty-foot shipping container for larger shipments.

The frame of the shelter is made of hundreds of CNC-cut notched slats, which when assembled and bolted together form a curved roof structure with flat faces on the front and the back. As

OPPOSITE

Shelter 2.0 is made from CNC cut parts and is available for anyone to download and build.

99

Bridges explains, the assembly process is akin to putting together a 3D wooden dinosaur puzzle. When assembled, the curved slats look like ribs and the horizontal structural members serve as interior shelves. Two doors and windows are inserted on either end to encourage cross ventilation and natural lighting. Only basic tools like wrenches and screwdrivers are necessary to assemble the shelter.

Bridges has found that an OSB product called AdvanTech is the best material to work with for CNC machining. It has low formaldehyde levels, is structurally very strong, and performs well in moist environments without degrading. Plastic sheeting, tarps, or sturdier materials like corrugated-metal panels can be used to enclose the structure. In the latter case, transparent plastic sheets are installed in place of two of the metal panels to allow more daylight into the structure. In total, the 10 x 14 foot shelter uses 27 sheets of ¾-inch and 11 sheets of ½-inch OSB, plus 27 sheets of corrugated metal, 2 sheets of transparent plastic, and 2 doors.

After the earthquake in Haiti, Bridges kicked his work into high gear and in the fall of 2010 raised enough money to build two shelters and ship them to colleagues working in the field on disaster recovery. He aimed to have ten more shelters delivered by the end of 2011. Bridges has also worked with local organizations on the East Coast to build two shelters for the homeless. One of those shelters went to a local man in Bridges's hometown of Exmore, Virginia, and the second was donated to the nonprofit housing organization Mad Housers, which is dedicated to providing shelter for the homeless and those in need of low-income housing. At the end of 2010, Bridges trucked a 10 x 14 foot shelter to Atlanta, Georgia, where he gave a demonstration of the assembly of his structure for the Mad Housers and then donated it to the organization so someone in need could live in it.

The beauty of Shelter 2.0 goes far beyond the physical nature of the shelter's design. Shelter 2.0's stated mission is to house 100 million homeless people. To achieve that ambitious goal, Bridges offers his designs for free to whoever wants them. On the Shelter 2.0 web site, the CNC files and instructions are available for download under a Creative Commons license, which allows anyone to use, modify, and build these shelters (as long as they give credit to Shelter 2.0 and don't sell them). Shelter 2.0 offers

LEFT

Assembly of Shelter 2.0 begins with laying the floor joists and raising the rips.

RIGHT

Cutting parts out of OSB on CNC machine for Shelter 2.0.

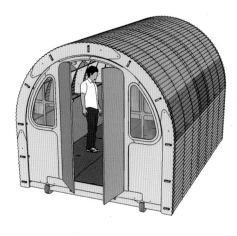

the plans for free but asks that those who do use them donate to the project. Of course, you can buy the shelters from Bridges for $2,900 each, but ideally, his goal is for as many people to make them as possible. Discussions with other CNC builders have already led to several improvements on the original Shelter 2.0 design, and Bridges hopes to continue this dialogue to further improve his design and create different models for different regions and climates.

Bridges also hopes that through his organization he can help educate people on CNC fabrication and put technology into the hands of the people who need it to build more homes. He would like other builders to upload their designs to the site for general use so that anyone who wants to build a shelter has the plans at his or her disposal. Shelter 2.0 is more than just a builder of disaster and homeless shelters; it is really an open-source portal where anyone interested in digitally fabricated shelters can get feedback, find collaborators, or source digital plans for shelters with the goal of housing as many people as possible.

TOP LEFT AND RIGHT
Assembling Shelter 2.0 for homeless man in Exmore, Virginia.

ABOVE LEFT
The front and back panels are inserted.

ABOVE RIGHT
Rendering of Shelter 2.0.

3.

AFFORDABLE HOUSING

Housing that can be built, bought, or rented by low-income families and that encourages energy-efficient and sustainable living.

Affordable housing is a term used for homes intended for families who earn less than the average income in their region. Sometimes referred to as "low-income housing," "subsidized housing," or "social housing," affordable housing denotes a home or apartment that can be bought or rented by a family at lower rates. As defined by HUD (US Department of Housing and Urban Development), "affordability" means that a family pays no more than 30 percent of their income on housing. Typically, government and nonprofit organizations like Habitat For Humanity in the US fund and construct these homes and either sell or rent them at reduced or subsidized costs. This is of course a great service to the low-income people in a given region and allows them to live close to their place of work.

The true range of what constitutes an affordable home is largely dependent on the country and the average income of an area. If looked at on a global level, billions of people need affordable housing, not just the 1 billion that live in slums. Affordable housing in the United States is not affordable in South Africa or India, and what is deemed acceptable in Pakistan may not even pass code in the UK. The term affordable is loosely defined here as achievable by those with lower incomes in a given country.

But regardless of the country, many elements of affordable housing are universal. Namely, all affordable housing should provide a respectable, quality, low-maintenance, and durable place to live. Design and construction of affordable housing should take into account the following elements:

1. **COST:** The overall cost to build the home or project, as well as the price at which units can be sold or rented, should be kept as low as possible.

2. **MATERIALS:** Ideally, materials should be locally sourced, low cost, and appropriate for the climate and culture.

3. **DURABILITY:** The home should be built for long-term wear and tear and take into account local climate conditions and disaster risk.

4. **MAINTENANCE:** The home should be designed to be low maintenance because low-income families have little money to spend on fixing or upgrading things that break down.

5. **ENERGY EFFICIENCY:** The more energy efficient a home is, the less a family must spend on heating, cooling, and electricity.

This section explores global solutions for affordable housing that go beyond subsidies and government aid. If we want to provide housing for the masses, we must examine methods that really do lower the costs of building maintenance, not just offer housing that costs the resident less to buy or rent. Affordability involves designing durable, smart homes, sourcing low-cost materials, and incorporating energy-efficient strategies to ensure that families have quality homes that will last them a lifetime. We must also teach these skills so that families are capable of building their own homes in the future.

PROJECT NAME
Gabion House

LOCATION
Lilavois, Haiti

ARCHITECT
Rafael Mattar-Neri

PROJECT TEAM
Hugh Brennan, Chris Howe,
Regan Potangaroa and
Rafael Mattar-Neri

BUILDER
Haven Partnership
(http://www.havenpartnership.com)

PARTNER ORGANIZATIONS
International Federation of Red Cross
and Red Crescent Societies
(http://www.ifrc.org) and Oxfam
America (http://www.oxfamamerica.org)

PROJECT YEAR
2011

PROJECT AREA
320 square feet

APPROXIMATE COST
$5,000

PHOTOS: Hugh Brennan

3.1

Gabion House

Debris from the Haiti earthquake is used as the building material to aid in the recovery process and construct affordable, earthquake- and hurricane-resistant homes.

The Haiti earthquake in January 2010 devastated Port-au-Prince and the surrounding towns, creating 19 million cubic meters of rubble and debris.[1] Before any rebuilding could begin, the rubble had to be cleared from the streets and building sites. But even a year after the disaster, thousands of people were still living in emergency and temporary shelters that provided little security and safety. One of the more critical factors of the reconstruction effort has been the lack of in-country resources with which to rebuild. What the country does have in large supply, though, is rubble from what is left of their concrete and masonry houses.

Many firms and organizations have proposed taking this debris and reusing it to build new, permanent, and more structurally sound homes.

One suggestion is to crush the debris to make aggregate for concrete; another solution involves filling gabion baskets with the rubble and using them as building blocks. Gabion baskets are wire cages that can be stacked and then packed with various materials like rock, aggregate, or masonry debris to form walls. Typically they are used for large infrastructure projects and retaining walls, but for Haiti they can be modified to erect load-bearing walls for energy-efficient homes. In the process of building these low-cost, permanent houses, people from the area are employed and debris is utilized, with the collateral benefit of alleviating the need to ship the rubble to the landfill.

In 2010, Haven Partnership joined efforts with Oxfam America and the International Federa-

OPPOSITE
Haitians give their approval of the
completed home.

tion of Red Cross and Red Crescent Societies to utilize the debris to build Gabion Houses on the outskirts of Port-au-Prince. Gabion baskets have been used before in building construction, but it is a not a very well-known technique. The Haven team, led by Hugh Brennan, sought to develop the construction methods, document the process, and prove that gabion baskets and rubble can be used to create a secure and healthy living environment. By the end of May 2011, the group had constructed one 255–square foot home in Croix-des-Bouquets and four 320–square foot homes in Lilavois.

The design for the Gabion House is largely based on traditional Haitian architecture, which is appropriate both culturally and climatically. A shaded veranda, where the inhabitants spend most of their time, is located at the entrance of a rectangular room covered with a large, pitched roof. The space is not totally closed in, permitting

TOP
Gabion House under construction in Lilavois, Haiti.

ABOVE LEFT
Rubble from surrounding damaged buildings was used to construct this home.

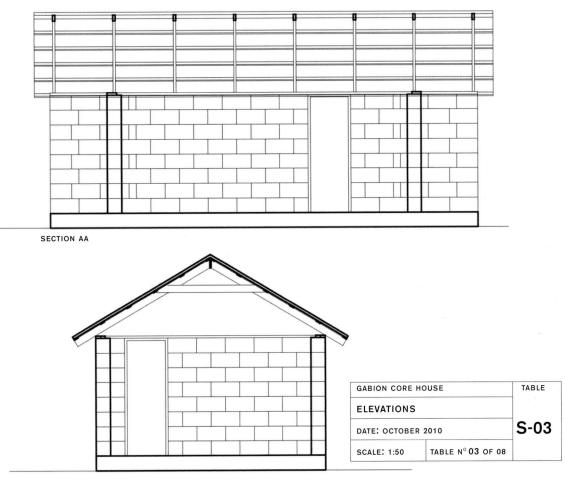

SECTION AA

SECTION BB

GABION CORE HOUSE		TABLE
ELEVATIONS		
DATE: OCTOBER 2010		**S-03**
SCALE: 1:50	TABLE N° 03 OF 08	

natural ventilation and allowing hot air to rise up and out of the space through vents on the gable ends. Basic, yet very functional and adaptable, the Gabion House is conceived as a core space with a window on either side that can be torn out to make way for new rooms or circulation routes if necessary.

Local people were hired to construct the homes. Only a moderate level of skill was required, much of which was taught on the job. First, the foundation is laid by filling a trench with crushed debris and then covering the debris with a layer of concrete made of locally crushed aggregate and sand. Next, women make the gabion baskets by cutting and shaping steel reinforcing mesh lined with chicken wire. The baskets are placed onto the wall, filled by hand with aggregate, and tied into place with wire both horizontally and vertically. Threaded steel bars connect the walls to the foundation, and corner bracing ensures that the structure is both hurricane and earth-

ABOVE
Elevations of the Gabion Home.

SIDE VIEW VERANDAH

FRONT VIEW VERANDAH

TOP VERANDAH

TOP

Renderings of the Gabion House.

ABOVE

Interior of the Gabion House.

ate size for the foundation, the baskets, or the fine-grain sand for the sand/cement render on the exterior. In the end, costs for a one-story Gabion House are running around $4,000–5,000 each. In addition to the low cost, the problem of debris removal is eliminated, and local people are employed, receive training, and are building their own permanent housing. The debris in the baskets also acts as a thermal buffer, protecting the interior from the heat of the sun and creating a cooler indoor enviroment. The Haven team has also worked diligently to ensure that the homes can be built to withstand hurricanes and earthquakes so that the people of Haiti never again have to endure destruction of that magnitude.

Haven and its partnering organizations are working to increase debris removal, purchase debris at a fair cost, and expand the processing of debris in order to build more houses. Training programs for the local labor force have been developed and are being adapted to suit the needs of the people, ensuring that the homes will be constructed correctly. With five houses already built, the project team hopes to build at least another hundred of them, as well as a two-story version in Haiti in the next few years.

quake resistant. Window and door openings are framed with lumber and then a trussed roof is installed. Two coats of a locally produced sand/cement render are applied to both the interior and exterior walls.

The costs of building the Gabion Houses are quite low, but can vary depending on the cost of local labor, the proximity to and cost of debris, and the quality of the rubble. Most of the labor is spent on crushing the debris to the appropri-

NOTE

1   "Haiti Earthquake Facts and Figures." Disasters Emergency Committee, 07 October 2010. Accessed 10 May 2011, http://www.dec.org .uk/haiti-earthquake-facts-and-figures.

TOP

The baskets are wired and connected together in such a way as to withstand seismic activity.

CENTER

The walls are completed and a sand/cement render coats the walls.

ABOVE

Roof trusses and roofing are added.

PROJECT NAME
SLUMtube

PROJECT TEAM
Andreas Claus Schnetzer and
Gregor Pils of Palettenhaus
(http://www.palettenhaus.com)

PROJECT AREA
645 square feet

LOCATION
Magagula Heights Township
near Johannesburg,
South Africa

PROJECT YEAR
2010

APPROXIMATE COST
Undetermined

PHOTOS: Palettenhaus

3.2

SLUMtube

Austrian architects take their knowledge of building with shipping pallets and teach South Africans how to construct warm and energy-efficient homes from found materials.

In South Africa, many people live in crudely erected shacks covered in found materials and corrugated metal. Summertime temperatures reach over 80 degrees F., while winter temperatures dip below 35 degrees F. With only a sheet of metal as protection, these shacks become very hot and very cold. Good materials for house construction abound, but education and tools to build homes that can protect against the elements and stay warm in winter and cool in summer, are sorely lacking.

In 2010, Austrian architects Andreas Claus Schnetzer and Gregor Pils, founding partners of Palettenhaus, traveled to the township of Magagula Heights, twenty-five miles outside of Johannesburg, South Africa. Schnetzer and Pils have built homes out of shipping pallets all over Europe

since 2008, one of which won the 2008 Gaudi European Student Competition on Sustainable Architecture. Their idea was that by using shipping pallets, a low-cost, often free material, they could help provide affordable housing for everyone, whether rich or poor. In South Africa, they put their knowledge of building with found materials to work and taught a group of local people how to construct safe and energy-efficient homes out of found materials.

As with the I-Beam Pallet House (see pages 71–73), the pallet is the building block of the structure and can be finished as desired, depending on the funds and materials available. Pallets are readily available in developing countries and can be acquired for practically nothing. Pallet houses can be insulated with straw, sand, or

any other locally available insulation material, and inexpensive plastic sheeting can be used for windows.

The pallet house becomes a means of self-help and could contribute to improving the social balance for the unemployed, the homeless, and those living in slums. In developing countries, shipping pallets are delivered filled with supplies, food, or other goods, but are then left to rot or are burned for heating or cooking. Schnetzer and Pils went to South Africa to show the people in the townships that they could build homes from shipping pallets, straw, clay, and found wood. Drawing on their plans from the rectangular Pallet House, they designed the SLUMtube, which is a more resource-efficient structure, requiring few tools and little skill to build.

TOP

Local children exploring the SLUMtube.

AOVE RIGHT

At one end of the SLUMtube, the pallets are fully exposed, showing the structural makeup of the tubular structure.

SLUMtube is a 645–square foot tubular structure with a room at each end and a common open space in the middle. Because wooden beams for construction are expensive and usually not of very good quality in South Africa and other developing countries, Schnetzer and Pils opted for a tubular design to eliminate the need for large beams. The basic structure is a double arc made out of shipping pallets and found wood and can be put up quickly. A covering of tarps, foil, and plastic sheeting provides protection from the elements.

After the structure was built, straw and clay were stuffed between the interior and exterior pallet slats to provide insulation. To make the structure even more energy efficient, the team finished off the exterior with a black covering topped by a

TOP
Interior courtyard at night.

ABOVE RIGHT
One of the residents cooking in the kitchen.

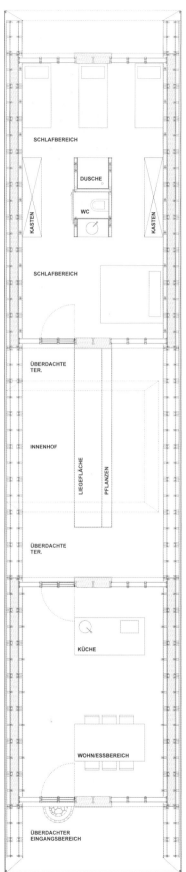

sheet of shiny corrugated metal. The metal covering is raised slightly above the surface to allow air
to pass underneath and keep the structure cool.

Inside the SLUMtube, one of the rooms is
elevated and contains the kitchen, living, and
dining areas. Old wooden beer crates are used for
tables and assorted storage. The middle, common area of the tube is open air to encourage

TOP LEFT

A kitty lounges on the
bench in the courtyard.

ABOVE LEFT

Construction of the SLUMtube
in process; stacks of pallets wait
to be put into use.

RIGHT

Floorplan of the SLUMtube.

They come in a standard shape, which makes the design for the SLUMtube universal. Using pallets is also environmentally beneficial; otherwise, the pallets are one-time use items, which end up in a landfill or are burned for heat. Straw, cellulose, sand, clay, newspaper, or any other locally available material can then be used to create insulation. By using found materials, the cost of the SLUMtube is practically nothing, which allows anyone who has the physical ability and time to build a home for themselves and their family. Training is required, though, to show people the basic principles of construction with pallets and how adding insulation can eliminate the need to burn pallets for heat.

The entire project took three months to complete and allowed the duo to test their theories and improve upon their design. Their new design requires only a handsaw and eliminates the need for screws and/or nails, which means that it could be built under any conditions, without power if necessary, and hopefully quicker. Because the design is universal, the SLUMtube can be adapted to local conditions very easily and at almost no cost. Schnetzer and Pils hope the SLUMtube can help alleviate the shortage and improve the quality of housing in slums and refugee camps around the world.

breezes to flow through the house. The other room is for sleeping and includes a boxed-in area with a toilet and a bath. Schnetzer and Pils's goal was to show the people that they could build out of almost any material they found.

Shipping pallets can easily be found anywhere in the world and are often free but may cost as much as $8 a pallet in developed countries.

TOP

The kitchen is constructed from found materials and reclaimed plastic crates.

ABOVE

The bedroom and bathroom.

PROJECT NAME
Pakistan Straw Bale and
Appropriate Building (PAKSBAB)
(http://www.paksbab.org)

LOCATION
Khyber Pakhtunkhwa,
Pakistan

PROJECT TEAM
Darcey Donovan and
Surkhab Khan

OWNER/CLIENT
Maziky Bibi

SEISMIC ENGINEERING
Network for Earthquake
Engineering Simulation
facility at the University
of Nevada, Reno

PROJECT YEAR
2010

PROJECT AREA
576 square feet

APPROXIMATE COST
$2,350

3.3

Pakistan Straw Bale and Appropriate Building

A U.S. nonprofit organization is training Pakistani people to build strong homes using regionally appropriate materials and bringing hope to an area demolished by the 2005 Kashmir earthquake and the floods of 2010.

The Kashmir earthquake in October 2005 killed more than 73,000 people and destroyed more than 600,000 homes, leaving 3.5 million people homeless.[1] After the floods of 2010, which the UN rates as the greatest humanitarian crisis in recent history, a good part of Pakistan has been reduced to a state of mud and rubble. In response to the earthquake, Pakistan Straw Bale and Appropriate Building (PAKSBAB) was founded in 2006 with the goal of helping the Pakistani people learn how to rebuild their homes and their lives. As of 2011, PAKSBAB had built twenty-three straw-bale homes and in the process trained hundreds of people in how to make use

of regionally appropriate materials and how to build seismically resistant homes that will remain standing even after the next major earthquake. This particular home was built for Maziky Bibi, her grandchildren, and daughter in-law, who lost their home in the earthquake.

After the Kashmir earthquake, Darcey Donovan, a licensed civil engineer with expertise in straw-bale homes and green building, responded to an e-mail from an earthquake relief volunteer requesting assistance to develop a straw-bale housing solution for northern Pakistan. Donovan helped design and build a one-room women's vocational training center out of straw bale in the earthquake-devastated village of Jabori. This structure proved that straw-bale construction could be implemented successfully and afford-

TOP

Installing beams at the top of the wall.

ABOVE LEFT

Laying the foundation with bags of gravel and netting.

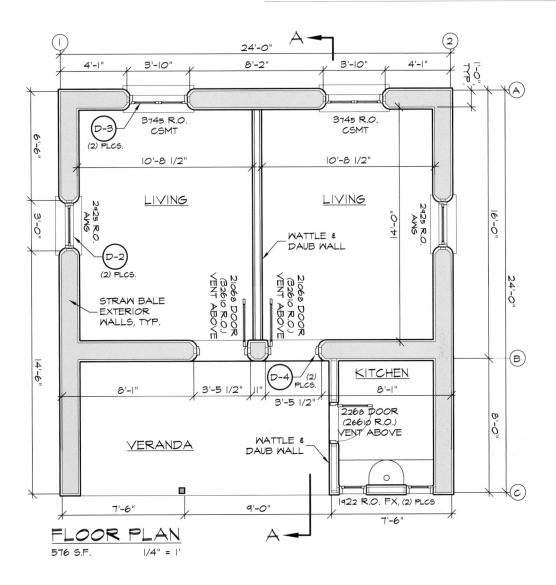

FLOOR PLAN

576 S.F.   1/4" = 1'

ably in Pakistan, so Donovan formed PAKSBAB and began developing unique straw-bale building methods that provide exceptional structural capacities at half the cost of conventional earthquake-resistant construction.

PAKSBAB's current straw-bale home design is 24 x 24 feet, with two rooms, a kitchen, and a veranda. The straw-bale walls both support the roof load and resist earthquake and wind loads, and this simple load-bearing design is what allows the homes to be built so inexpensively. The foundation consists of a layer of gravel-filled bags covered with soil cement. The straw bales are laid on top of the foundation; bamboo pins help to keep the walls plumb during construction and to resist loads. Lightweight roofs of wooden trusses or I-beams are covered in corrugated

ABOVE

Floorplan of the PAKSBAB straw bale house.

metal and insulated with light clay and straw. A nylon fishing net is spread underneath the foundation, then wrapped up and over the walls, providing a surface for the plaster reinforcement to adhere to and tying the foundation, straw-bale walls, and roof together.

Earthen plaster coats the interior and exterior walls, encasing the straw bales and providing additional structural support, as well as aesthetic qualities. Many owners paint their new homes with a lime wash and finish the interior floor with a layer of soil cement and linseed oil. Gutters are installed on the edge of the roof to collect rainwater for household use.

In 2009, PAKSBAB built a test model home and placed it on a shake table at the Network for Earthquake Engineering Simulation facility at the University of Nevada, Reno, to determine its seismic response. The home survived extensive testing and earthquake simulations without collapsing. Although it was damaged, the tests proved that the PAKSBAB design was adequate to withstand seismic activity greater than that of the 2005 Kashmir earthquake. PAKSBAB took the lessons learned from this testing to improve upon their design and get official approval from

building authorities. In addition, the home demonstrated that the earthen plaster, made up of clay and chopped straw, is very fire resistant in a one-hour ASTM (American Society for Testing and Materials) fire test.

Straw bales appropriate for construction were not readily available in Pakistan, so PAKSBAB had to develop a system to fabricate the bales on site. The organization utilizes locally fabricated

LEFT	TOP RIGHT	ABOVE RIGHT
Final coat of plaster is applied.	Compressing loose straw into straw bales.	No one in Pakistan makes straw bales like in the US, so the bales have to be handmade.

compression molds and manually operated farm jacks to create the bales, which are smaller than those traditionally used in the U.S. The straw is sourced locally and now provides a new means of income for farmers and landowners.

Typical reconstruction of homes in the region has involved energy-intensive, scarce, and expensive materials like reinforced concrete and confined masonry. In contrast to PAKSBAB straw-bale homes, these conventional homes tend to perform poorly in extreme weather conditions, and unless they are constructed properly to code, they will come crashing down on the inhabitants in the next earthquake. Moreover, PAKSBAB builds their straw-bale homes very inexpensively. Each home requires about 300 straw bales and about 1,200 hours of labor. At this time, the laborers work for free in exchange for training, so the cost of the home is for the materials only, which comes to around $2,350, or about $4 per square foot.

The homes rely on energy-efficient and passive solar design to keep the residents comfortable throughout the year. Straw bales not only serve as load-bearing members but also provide a high level of insulation, which, coupled with the roof insulation, keeps the homes cool in the summer and warm in the winter. PAKSBAB is also educating the local population about passive solar design, rainwater catchment, high-efficiency cooking and heating, compost toilets, and the use of natural building materials.

The organization's goal is to improve the lives of the poor. The recipients of the straw-bale homes have been victims of the earthquake or the floods, or are widows with children. Construction of the homes is always coupled with extensive training for the homes' inhabitants and other locals. PAKSBAB is currently working on a construction field guide that can be distributed to people in the region to promote safe and regionally appropriate construction. The organization is also working to set up microfinancing to help the poor finance home construction. Eventually, PAKSBAB hopes to extend their home design and construction methods beyond Pakistan's borders to help other developing countries.

NOTES

1 "Pakistan Earthquake—Oct 2005." Pakistan Earthquake Reconstruction & Rehabilitation Authority. Accessed 25 January 2011, http://www.erra.pk/eq2005.asp.

LEFT

Laying the roofing material on the roof, which is insulated with more strawbale.

RIGHT

Maziky Bibi and her family in front of their new home.

PROJECT NAME
CasaChica

LOCATION
San Sebastián La Cañada,
Morelos, Mexico

PROJECT TEAM
Juan Casillas Pintor,
Guillermo Galindo Reyes
of Laboratorio
Arquitectura Básica Mx
(http://labmx.blogspot.com)

CONSULTANTS & PARTNERS
Arq. Juan Pablo Wolffer, Arq.
Felipe Creel, Ms. Anaïs Desrieux

CONTRACTOR
Andrés García

PROJECT YEAR
2010

PROJECT AREA
678 square feet

APPROXIMATE COST
$25,000

PHOTOS: Laboratorio Aquitectura Básica MX

3.4

CasaChica

A compact house in rural Mexico takes advantage of natural resources and local materials to find appropriate and affordable building solutions.

A young couple from Mexico City decided they wanted a simpler way of life, so they moved to their family's property south of the capital to find an alternative way of living. They hired Laboratorio Arquitectura Básica Mx to help them design and build a small home that made use of local and natural resources from the area. The result was CasaChica (small house), and it is more than just a home with a small environmental impact. The little straw-bale home was also an exploration into responsible architecture and a community project to help educate local people on better and lower-impact construction.

By now, Laboratorio Arquitectura Básica Mx has built some twenty-five rural projects, including clinics, libraries, schools, and straw-bale buildings. They have even built a home using waste materials for insulation and shipping pallets for walls. The goal of their firm is to find appropriate architectural solutions for basic human needs like clean air, pure water, healthy food, affordable housing, and good education in order to have a positive impact on the planet and their community. Reliance on local resources, sustainable design, and community involvement is key to their success. It was with these principles and ideals that the firm tackled the design and construction of this small rural home in central Mexico.

Most of the home was built with local materials like clay, straw, stone, and bamboo. Construction was completed in ten months with the help of family, friends, local labor, and weekend construction workshops conducted by the firm. CasaChica is an infill straw-bale house with

OPPOSITE

CasaChica makes use of locally available materials and is appropriately designed for the region.

a stone-and-mortar foundation, plaster walls, and a steel-framed roof. At a mere 678 square feet, it has little room for anything but the necessities. One all-purpose space serves as living room, dining room, and bedroom; a partial wall in the center of the space partitions off a kitchenette, and a large deck (not yet constructed) serves as the outdoor living area. In the back, a sink separates a toilet room and a shower stall. Throughout, built-in shelves and cabinets provide storage. A gap between the thick straw-bale walls and the roof opens the entire house to the outdoors, and its partially shaded site keeps the house cool even on the hottest of days.

After the initial plan for the home had been determined, the footprint was excavated and all the clay reserved for later use. A stone foundation rising three feet above the ground level was laid,

and six cement-block columns were erected at the corners and in the center of the side walls. Next, steel beams were laid on top of the columns and a welded butterfly-roof frame was installed. Unlike most roofs in Mexico and developing countries around the world, which are made of corrugated metal sheeting, CasaChica's roof is earth insulated. Wood planks were laid for the ceiling, which was then covered with four inches of clay and straw, a layer of chicken wire, and finally a thin layer of cement mortar topped with a water-resistant coating. The butterfly roof is angled toward a central gutter, which directs water into a nearby 18,500-gallon tank.

Once the roof was installed, Laboratorio Arquitectura Básica Mx conducted a community workshop to teach locals how to build with straw bales. The participants in the workshop installed

ABOVE

CasaChica almost complete.

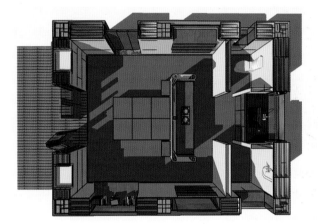

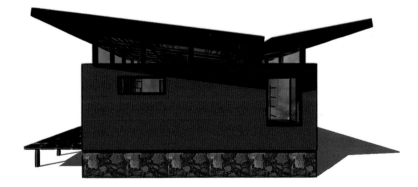

TOP

Floorplan of the CasaChica
home.

MIDDLE

Cross section of CasaChica.

ABOVE

Rendering of CasaChica
from the side.

locally sourced straw bales onto the foundation, framed out the windows and doors, and then covered the interior and exterior walls with clay plaster. All of the clay used to plaster the walls came from the soil excavated for the foundation. Next they built the interior walls out of bamboo, which is commonly found in the region; in this case it was sourced from a neighbor's property. Instead of receiving money for the bamboo, the neighbors bartered it for the entire harvest of one plum tree found in CasaChica's garden. The bamboo walls were covered in clay plaster for a smooth finish. Finally, electricity and water were installed, and the entire house was painted with a natural paint made from lime and cactus.

As the home is completely open to the outdoors because of the gap between the roof and the walls, natural ventilation, shading, and the thick

TOP

Installing straw bales on the foundation and in between the support beams.

ABOVE LEFT

Framed window in a straw bale wall.

straw-bale walls keep it cool and comfortable. Rainwater and wastewater from the sink and shower are used to irrigate the garden next to the house. A solar hot-water system heats water, and the home needs very little additional energy—for lights and cooking only. The use of mostly local materials and a design geared specifically to the local climate ensure that this small home has a low environmental impact.

But CasaChica is much more than an environmentally sensitive home. It's also an excellent educational tool for the local people, who think that concrete construction is the only way to go. This little home, made from very inexpensive local materials, is an amazing example of what homes in the region and even in other countries could be. Mexico, a major exporter of grain, has plenty of straw, which is usually burned but could be utilized to make energy-efficient, comfortable homes. Laboratorio Arquitectura Básica Mx wants to address the lack of housing in rural Mexico by using straw bales and clay in combination with local and commercial materials like cement and steel. It takes community workshops like the one organized for CasaChica to help educate people about alternative construction methods and the integration of local materials with existing methods.

TOP

The open air home stays cool because of the natural ventilation.

ABOVE

Bamboo poles were used for the interior walls, which were then plastered over.

PROJECT NAME
Bone House

LOCATION
Huntsville, Texas, USA

PROJECT TEAM
Phoenix Commotion
(http://www.phoenixcommotion.com)

ARCHITECT
Dan Phillips

PROJECT YEAR
2011

PROJECT AREA
750 square feet

APPROXIMATE COST
$52,200

3.5

Bone House

Texas homebuilder Dan Phillips makes use of leftovers, scraps, and reclaimed materials to build affordable, energy-efficient homes while training workers in construction.

"Repetition creates pattern" is the mantra of homebuilder Dan Phillips, who started a building initiative, the Phoenix Commotion, in his hometown of Huntsville, Texas. A visionary in many ways and even a bit on the radical side, Phillips takes the waste, scraps, and leftover materials of the building industry and creates unique, organic, low-maintenance, and energy-efficient homes for the working poor. He employs unskilled workers to help him build the homes; in the process, they gain skills and go on to higher-paying jobs. The owners of the homes are also required to help build the home, which instills a sense of pride and makes them appreciate their home more. So not only is Phillips creating affordable homes, he's also adding value to his community through education and honest labor.

Phillips began his home construction company in 1997 as a way to correct the imbalance between perfectly good building materials going to the landfills and the shocking lack of affordable housing. By 2011, Phillips and his company, named after the mythical bird that rises from the ashes, have built around two dozen projects, mostly in the Huntsville area. Not everyone can have a home built by Phoenix Commotion though, and Phillips has a hierarchy for deciding whom to build for. His preference is for single mothers, followed by low-income families and then artists.

One of the more recent projects to be completed is the Bone House, a three-bedroom home and working studio for three local artists in the center of Huntsville. The home was built as a way

wine-bottle-cork flooring, and cedar siding on both the interior and the exterior. Each artist has his own room and bathroom and shares a kitchen/living room and garden space.

Construction of the original home began in 2007, but it tragically burned to the ground in 2010. It was completely rebuilt and finally completed in 2011. Though 750 square feet may seem small for three people, Phillips keeps his homes small to minimize material usage and maximize energy efficiency. He compensates for the small interior space with a lot of outdoor living space and decks, as Texas enjoys pleasant weather for most of the year.

to support the local arts community, and the residents all had to have a legitimate portfolio in order to rent space there. As the name of the house suggests, bone is used throughout for both decorative and functional purposes. Bones, which were gathered from nearby ranches and are not as creepy as one might think, appear in railings, trim, tiles, door handles, and more. Other features of the eclectic home include beer-bottle-cap tiles, mosaic tile and mirror showers,

Most of Phoenix Commotions' houses are 600–800 square feet and are designed to live lightly on the earth, owing to their small footprint and energy-efficient features. All of the homes feature high-efficiency insulation, rainwater catchment systems, solar hot water or tankless water heaters and high-efficiency heat pumps. The homes meet or exceed local or national building codes and usually cost around $30–40 per square foot in materials, plus the cost of labor. Phillips's work-

TOP LEFT
One of three bedrooms in the Bone House.

ABOVE
Stairway to the second floor.

TOP RIGHT
Bones are used all over the house for decoration.

ers are unskilled for the most part, paid minimum wage, and hired as part of a building training program for a year, after which Phillips pushes them on to find higher-paying jobs.

Each home is quite unique and is designed and built through a very organic process, which is largely dependent on the materials Phillips comes across. As Phillips builds a home, he sticks to two general rules. First, good design must be part of the process, that is, materials can't just be thrown in at random. Second, and most important, there has to be a pattern. Broken tiles may not be good enough to use in a high-end home, but in a Phoenix Commotion home, a lot of broken tiles create a pattern. Bottle caps and corks don't seem like much individually, but when you have a lot of them, they create a beautiful mosaic floor. Materials are sourced from a variety of locations, including the dump, wholesalers, friends, remodelers discarding things, building scraps, and much more.

For the most part, the materials are free; after fourteen years, Phillips has become quite the scavenger for usable building materials, and people often donate materials to him. In fact, Phillips has helped start a number of building-material exchanges around Texas to help minimize the quantity of construction materials being sent to the landfill. Though most of his homes are built from scraps and recycled or reclaimed materials, Phillips does insist on buying some things new to ensure quality, efficiency, and durability, including wiring, plumbing, insulation, nails, screws, adhesives, and faucets.

Incorporating reused and reclaimed materials into a home takes a lot of patience and planning. It is certainly not as easy as driving to your local big-box home-improvement store and picking up the materials you need, but it is a much more sustainable—and affordable—practice. Phillips knows that the type of work he does will never become mainstream, especially using bone as decoration, but his goal is that through demonstration and advocacy he can show that it is, in fact, a viable model.

LEFT

Eclectic tiled shower, sink, and bathroom floor.

RIGHT

The artists' studio.

PROJECT NAME
10x10 Housing at Freedom
Park

LOCATION
Cape Town, South Africa

LEAD ARCHITECT
Luyanda Mpahlwa of
DesignSpaceAfrica, formerly
of MMA Architects (http://www
.designspaceafrica.com)

PROJECT TEAM
Sushma Patel, Uli Mpahlwa,
Kirsty Ronne, Westley van Wyk

ENGINEERING CONSULTANT
Henry Herring, AKI

SURVEYORS
Brian Mahachi, BTKM Quantity
Surveyors

BUILDING TECHNOLOGY
Mike Trenmere, EcoBuild
Technologies (http://www
.ecobuildtechnologies.com)

BUILDING CONTRACTOR
Schalk van der Walt,
Tech Homes

PARTNER ORGANIZATION
Design Indaba
(http://www.designindaba.com)

PROJECT YEAR
2009

PROJECT AREA
580 square feet

APPROXIMATE COST
each project: $7,860-8,464
(R65,000-70,000); $78,979-
85,055 (R650,000–700,000)

PHOTOS: Wieland Gleich – ARCHIGRAPHY.com, courtesy
of Luyanda Mpahlwa DesignSpaceAfrica

3.6

10x10 Housing at Freedom Park

Traditional building techniques and advanced building technologies come together in this low-cost housing project in South Africa.

To help address the shortage of affordable housing in South Africa, Design Indaba, a local organization dedicated to improving the world through design, issued a challenge to ten local architects, asking them to come up with creative solutions for low-cost housing. These ten teams worked on a pro bono basis to develop affordable, innovative, sustainable, and energy-efficient designs that would also help change the perception of low-cost housing. Homes for the 10x10 Low-Cost Housing Project were awarded via a lottery to eligible families in Freedom Park at Cape Flats south of Cape Town. Initially, the homes were to be 40 square meters in size and cost less than the government subsidy of R50,000 per household.

The first ten of these homes to be built were designed by Luyanda Mpahlwa, formerly of MMA Architects and now principal of his own firm, DesignSpaceAfrica. Mpahlwa's goal for the project was to offer dignified housing and a better quality of life for families in Freedom Park. He wanted to address the quality of low-cost housing in general while simultaneously exploring sustainable and appropriate design. Many people in South Africa and other developing countries around the world view brick-and-mortar construction as the standard and best way to build, but Mpahlwa hoped to change that perception by reinstituting more traditional techniques with regionally appropriate materials.

Mpahlwa and his team were presented with ten plots of land on which to design and build their houses. The lots were small (112 square meters; 1,206 square feet), so the decision was made to maximize the space by building two-story houses, thus minimizing the footprint and allowing more space for a garden. Living spaces, including a living room, kitchen, and bathroom, were located on the lower floor; two bedrooms and an attached deck on the upper. Mpahlwa conceived these houses as "starter homes," complete with the basic amenities but capable of being expanded as needed, when money was available. The homes front the street and are situated on the lots to make the most of the garden space and allow for rooms to be added on in back.

To achieve affordability for this type of housing, an efficient building system had to be imple-mented. Mpahlwa and his team settled on the timber and sandbag EcoBeam system by Eco-Build Technologies, designed and manufactured in Cape Town. Each structural beam consists of two timber boards with a metal inlay, which are prefabricated to the exact length needed for the home's construction. Easily transportable polycarbonate bags are filled with sand on site and stacked to form the walls of the building. Prefabricated window- and doorframes, also made by EcoBuild Technologies, are inserted into the appropriate spaces with transparent polycarbonate panels serving as windows. The interior walls are finished with timber boarding over the sandbags.

After the structure is built, the exterior is covered in chicken wire and plastered to create a hard, reinforced cement finish, which is then

TOP LEFT

Laying the sand bag foundation.

TOP RIGHT

Exterior of one of the homes partially plastered.

ABOVE

Filling sandbags into wall systems.

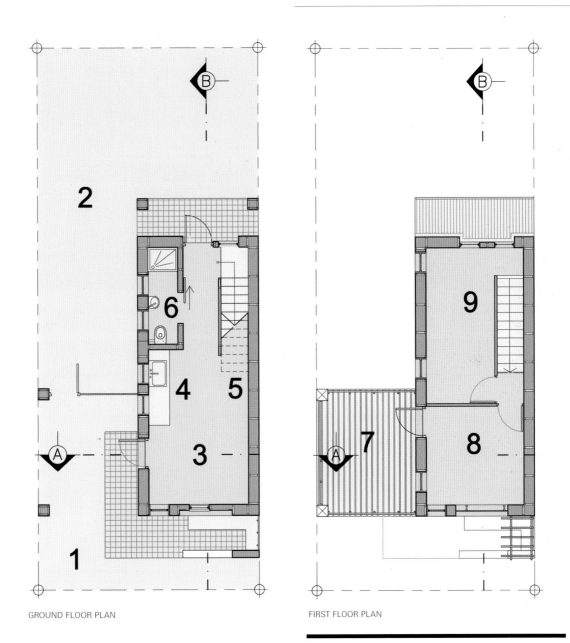

GROUND FLOOR PLAN

FIRST FLOOR PLAN

LEGEND

1	ENTRANCE	**6**	BATHROOM
2	GARDEN	**7**	BALCONY
3	LIVING ROOM	**8**	MASTER BEDROOM
4	KITCHENETTE	**9**	BEDROOM 2
5	DINING/STUDY		

ABOVE

Floorplans of Freedom Park houses.

brightly painted. Like wattle and daub construction, the sandbags provide excellent thermal mass, collecting heat during the day and releasing it at night, and keeping the interior cool in summer and retaining the heat in winter. The plaster finish serves as a rain screen, and any water that does get through is filtered down to the ground by the sand.

The unique system is well suited for mass production and unskilled labor. In fact, many women were a part of the construction crew, and all

---

TOP LEFT

Starting on the second floor of one of the homes.

TOP RIGHT

Luyanda Mpahlwa, the architect, checking on the progress of the homes.

ABOVE

The upstairs deck provides extra outdoor living space, but could easily be turned into another bedroom.

of the laborers needed only a couple of days to master the methods. The only part of the home's construction that required skilled labor was the application of the plaster exterior. Otherwise, all of the materials were sourced or produced nearby and local construction jobs benefited the economically depressed area. There was also no need for electricity during the construction of these homes. While the homes ended up costing more than the original budget, Design Indaba and Mpahlwa determined that economies of scale would drive the price down, bringing the cost of these homes directly in line with the government allowance of R50,000.

Luyanda Mpahlwa and his team received the inaugural Curry Stone Design Prize, administered by the Universityof Kentucky College of Design, in September 2008 for their Design Indaba 10x10 House. This annual international prize recognizes breakthrough design solutions with the power and potential to improve our lives and the world we live in. Construction of the homes was completed in the summer of 2009 and soon thereafter ten families moved into their new energy-efficient, sustainably designed homes.

ABOVE

The homes were designed as 'starter homes', but can easily be added on to as needed.

PROJECT NAME
Birchway Eco-Community
(http://www.birchwayeco.com)

LOCATION
Hayes, UK

ARCHITECT
Acanthus LW Architects
(http://www.acanthuslw.co.uk)

DEVELOPER
Paradigm Housing
(http://paradigmhousing.co.uk)

STRATEGIC PARTNERS
London Borough of Hillingdon

MANUFACTURERS
FutureForm by Tingdene
(http://www.futureformltd.com)

CONSTRUCTION PARTNERS
Sunrise Hotels Ltd
(http://www.epsilonmanagement.co.uk)

FUNDING
The Homes and Communities Agency
(HCA)

PROJECT YEAR
2010

PROJECT AREA
14,369 square feet

APPROXIMATE COST
$8,471,533 (£5,399,620)

PHOTOS: Paradigm Housing Group 2009 (unless otherwise indicated)

3.7

Birchway Eco-Community

Prefabricated, green-roofed housing creates an
affordable and eco-friendly community outside of London.

A building site in Hayes, England was slated for a
low-rent housing project; to appease the neighbors, who would be losing their views of green
space, the developer wanted to make sure the
project maximized vegetation. The unusual long
and narrow L-shaped site required innovative
solutions as well as forward-thinking, sustainable design. The result is an affordable housing
project comprising five low-rise block apartment
buildings with one- and two-bedroom apartments covered in arched green roofs. The average
rent for the apartments is £100 a week.

Paradigm Housing Group, a housing and services provider in the greater London area, led
the charge to build these flats in the borough of
Hillingdon, northwest of London. Acanthus LW,
a UK firm, was asked to design the low-cost

housing project. From the beginning, Paradigm
and Acanthus had three very important goals
for the Birchway Eco-Community: minimal
impact, sustainability, and the use of "Modern
Methods of Construction." First, they sought
to minimize the impact of the new development
on the surrounding homes and neighbors. The
site was considered a "backland" site, meaning
that it was bordered on either side by back-
yards, and the neighbors were none too happy
about the potential loss of their green backyard
views. Previous attempts to develop the odd
property had failed with the planning commission because the developers hadn't taken the
neighbors into consideration. To alleviate the
neighbors' concerns, Paradigm and Acanthus
were determined to maximize the greenery and
keep the overall height of the buildings down.

OPPOSITE
A green-roofed Birchway Eco Home.

From these objectives, the idea of the green roof emerged.

The second goal was to achieve the highest levels of sustainability possible within the given budget. In the beginning, the design team sought to achieve Level 4 of the UK Code for Sustainable Homes, but upon review, Paradigm decided to strive for Level 5 in order to achieve a carbon-neutral development.[1] Birchway Eco-Community is the first social housing project in London to achieve the highest level of the code. After seeking additional funding to boost the green strategies, Paradigm was able to meet the government's goal for all housing to be carbon neutral by 2016, six years ahead of schedule.

Finally, the last goal for the development was to make use of Modern Methods of Construction, or MMS, which is essentially highly controlled, prefabricated, modular construction. Utilizing MMS allows for a much more accelerated construction schedule and better quality control, which leads to improved energy efficiency. FutureForm, a division of Tingdene, handled all the prefabrication in their factory in Northampton.

The modules for the twenty-four apartments were fabricated out of 65 percent recycled steel in just a few weeks and were delivered to the site with all services and fittings built in, including kitchens and bathrooms. Sunrise Hotels Ltd took over from there and installed the modules in a matter of days to complete the homes. Overall, fabrication and on-site finish work took about three months, which is considerably faster than traditional construction. This minimized the impact on the neighbors, reduced material wastage, and ensured that each home was built according to the specifications set for energy efficiency.

A high standard of thermal insulation and air-tightness, combined with heat-recovery ventilation systems, minimizes energy use for heating and cooling. Energy for heating and hot water is generated by a biomass central wood chip boiler.

LEFT

Installation of the prefabricated modules.

RIGHT

Renderings of the Birchway Eco Community.

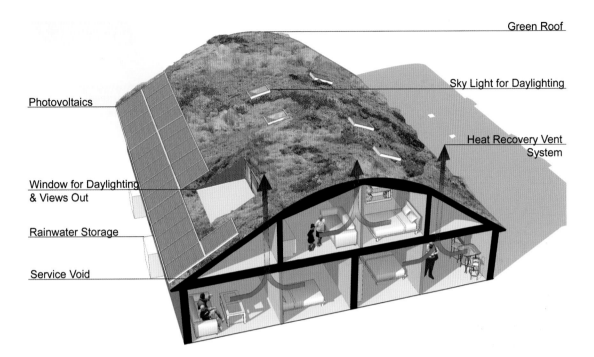

Green Roof

Sky Light for Daylighting

Heat Recovery Vent System

Photovoltaics

Window for Daylighting & Views Out

Rainwater Storage

Service Void

The exterior of the buildings is clad in brick and timber, and the arched roofs are entirely covered in sedum, a drought-tolerant plant. Skylights punctuate the arched roofs, drawing sunlight down into the first-floor apartments, and photovoltaic systems line the south side of the rooflines to produce the rest of the building's energy.

The green roof is completely covered in sedum planted in soil over a waterproof membrane and improves insulation, helps filter pollutants, minimizes storm water runoff, acts as a sound barrier, and encourages wildlife. Rainwater is harvested from the green roof and used for toilet flushing. The rest of the landscaping was planned to encourage biodiversity and ecological activity. Interior and exterior materials were chosen for their environmental responsibility, and recycling and composting facilities are provided on site.

Birchway Eco-Community, now called Greenwood Close, is more than just an environmentally friendly development and affordable housing project; it is also a community and a teaching tool. When renters move into their new apartment, they are given a Home Owners Guide and an opportunity to sign a green charter, which is a set of green standards by which to live. The guide and voluntary charter help the residents reduce their environmental impact, energy and water usage, and waste. Tips are regularly provided for healthier and more sustainable living, and the residents are encouraged to participate in projects and start gardens. The residents' green charter is a unique resident-focused initiative launched by Paradigm to encourage the new occupants to buy into a better, greener way of living.

NOTES

1   UK Code for Sustainable Homes, http://www. planningportal.gov.uk/buildingregulations/ greenerbuildings/sustainablehomes

ABOVE
Diagram of the sustainable features of the Birchway buildings. (Acanthus LW)

PROJECT NAME
Urban Tulou

LOCATION
Nanhai, Guangdong, China

ARCHITECT
Urbanus Architecture & Design
(http://www.urbanus.com.cn)

GENERAL CONTRACTOR
Shenzhen Jiasheng Architecture
Construction Co., Ltd

LDI STRUCTURE/MEP
Archilier Architecture LLC

DEVELOPER
Vanke Estate Co., Ltd

PROJECT YEAR
2008

PROJECT AREA
147,584 square feet

APPROXIMATE COST
$6,474,334
(41,133,000 yuan)

3.8

Urban Tulou

Traditional Chinese architecture inspires a new urban typology of low-income housing in Guangdong Province.

Sometimes it takes a lesson from history to build homes for the future, which is exactly what the Chinese architecture firm Urbanus did to design and build a modern, urban, and low-income housing project in the Nanhai district of Guangdong Province in southern China. Urban Tulou is directly inspired by the traditional fortresslike apartment buildings of China's Hakka minority in Fujian Province. Completed in 2008, Urban Tulou is serving as an experiment in communal and affordable housing, and may soon be replicated to provide more housing for the swelling migrant-worker populations in rapidly growing Chinese cities.

The tulou is a traditional communal residential building, built between the twelfth and twentieth centuries from brick, wood, and rammed earth,

usually in a circular configuration but sometimes in a square around a central courtyard. Originally built to provide a strong defense against marauders, the communal living quarters have very thick walls (up to six feet) with only one heavily barred entrance and exit on the ground floor and windows on the top floors from which inhabitants could defend themselves. Each tulou was designed so that the inhabitants could safely lock the gate and have enough food, water, and supplies to last until the invaders gave up and left. In fact, many of the tulous had integrated water and sewage systems to maintain the inhabitants' health even during a siege.

Three or four stories of living quarters surround a central courtyard often featuring a shrine or other buildings. Some tulous are quite large in

OPPOSITE

Exterior of Urban Tulou and one of the entrances.

diameter and house up to eight hundred people, who are usually part of the same clan or family and everyone lives as equals. There are thousands of tulous still standing in southern China, and in 2008 a number of these clusters were awarded World Heritage Site status by UNESCO as a testament to their construction and continued functionality for communal living. They are praised for their ability to withstand earthquakes and strong wind, are well ventilated, are naturally daylit, and remain cool in summer and warm in winter.

Urbanus took many lessons from this vernacular architecture, especially with regard to natural lighting, ventilation, durability, and equality. Many of these elements, particularly the general circular form, were retained, but designing for a modern culture and rapidly growing population raises some challenges, so Urbanus had to expand upon the idea of the tulou to make it appropriate for today's world.

First, with an average diameter of 50 meters (104 feet), traditional tulous could house many families, but modern tulous need to house even more. Urban Tulou is 72 meters (236 feet) in diameter, 6 stories high, and designed to house 1,860 people in 287 apartments with an updated configuration that includes a central block building to maximize space.

Second, the modern tulou is not a defensible fortress meant to keep out intruders. Though privacy, peace, and quiet are certainly important in rapid-paced urban environments, the building also needs to be open, accessible, and welcoming. Rather than closing off the building with only

The rooftop of the innner apartment block provides recreation space for the residents.

The ground floor provides space for the community, restaurants and businesses.

one entrance, there are multiple ground-floor entrances, and exterior windows provide more daylighting than their historic counterparts. The exterior features narrow balconies covered in a prefab concrete screen and wooden shutters to provide security and shade and encourage ventilation.

Third, while rammed earth is an exceptional building material, on a large scale it is not practical or economically feasible. Therefore, Urban Tulou is constructed from precast concrete and steel, which are both cheaper and easier.

Urban Tulou acts as a village within a city, providing community, amenities, retail space, restaurants, and even jobs. Those who have jobs in the tulou enjoy smaller private apartments, while

TOP

View of the interior courtyard.

ABOVE RIGHT

An outdoor patio provides space for residents to gather and be out of their apartment.

families and groups of migrant workers share larger apartments. Rent for each apartment is designed to stay low, around 600–700 yuan (US $90–100) per month, so that even the lowest-paid citizen can afford to have decent accommodations. The apartments are small by Western standards (30 square meters; 323 square feet), but are efficient and designed with built-in storage and multifunctional spaces and furniture like balconies for drying laundry and beds that fold away during the day. Additionally, there are lots of public areas available to the residents, including a billiards hall, fitness area, sports courts, computer room, courtyards, and more, so that they can get out of their apartment to interact with other people.

Urban Tulou is an experiment in low-income urban housing and very unique in a city full of high-rise buildings. The airy, circular building, inspired by the fortresslike buildings of historic China, is re-envisioned for a modern world where decent housing is out of reach for the average person. Urbanus hopes to expand upon the original prototype and construct more throughout the country to alleviate the housing shortage.

TOP RIGHT

The living room in one of the apartments.

ABOVE RIGHT

The apartments are small, but efficiently designed and feature built-in storage.

4.

PREFAB HOUSING

A home that is partially or entirely built off site, transported to the site, and then assembled and completed.

A prefab or prefabricated home is one that is either partially or entirely constructed and fabricated off site, typically in a warehouse, and then put together after it has been transported to the site. Prefab housing has been around in various forms for almost a century and is praised for its efficient use of materials, fast construction, quality control, and ability to achieve economies of scale.

Until the last decade or so, prefab homes were primarily associated with modular and trailer homes built for quantity over quality, but in recent years the green building movement has adopted prefab housing as one of the leading solutions to provide efficient, sustainable housing for the masses. Because the homes or their parts are built in a factorylike setting, weather does not hinder the construction and quality can be controlled, resulting in faster construction time and an overall better product. Additionally, thanks to smart design, homes can be built with a tighter, more energy-efficient envelope that reduces the need for heating and cooling after the home is built.

Prefab housing is a broad term and may also be referred to as kit homes, modular housing, or container homes. Materials used to build prefab homes vary widely and include Structural Insulated Panels (SIPs), straw bales, steel frames, shipping containers, premade wall systems, Insulated Concrete Forms (ICFs), and more. The point of prefab construction is to build cost-effective homes efficiently and on a large scale. Design and construction of affordable prefab housing should take into account the following:

1. **COST:** Economies of scale can be reached by buying materials in bulk and mass-producing the end product.

2. **MATERIALS:** Building inside a factory improves resource management and reduces waste better than building on site.

3. **FABRICATION:** A controlled factory setting allows construction to happen faster and even during inclement weather.

4. **DELIVERY:** The home should be designed around cost-effective delivery methods such as flat-packing materials, wall systems, and prefabricated parts or even shipping the entire house on the back of a truck.

5. **ASSEMBLY:** Upon arrival at the site, parts are usually assembled in weeks rather than months, as in traditional construction.

This section takes a look at a number of different prefab construction methods for both single-family homes and larger developments. Though few manufacturers of prefab homes have attained the economies of scale to make the system profitable and more affordable, there are enough advantages to make prefab a serious contender as a housing solution on a large scale. In time, treating homes as factory-built products like cars or TVs will drive down their overall cost and build them much faster than traditional methods. Materials, strategies, and designs vary widely but can be adjusted to match the climate and vernacular architecture of a given site in order for the homes to be widely accepted and eventually more affordable. Prefab construction is likely to become the fastest and most cost-effective way to build houses for our rapidly growing population.

PROJECT NAME
Land Yacht

PROJECT TEAM
Reclaimed Space
(http://reclaimedspace.com)

PROJECT AREA
512 square feet

LOCATION
Outside of Austin, Texas, USA

PROJECT YEAR
2010

APPROXIMATE COST
$78,000

PHOTOS: John Pettyjohn

4.1

Land Yacht

Reclaimed wood salvaged from an old brewery is transformed into a prefabricated cabin in rural Texas.

In between construction jobs in 2007, Texas rancher and builder Tracen Gardner came up with the idea of building small, easily transportable structures out of reclaimed materials. With a plethora of dilapidated, abandoned barns on nearby farms and ranches, Gardner knew he had a vast supply of salvageable wood from which he could build his structures. In 2008, Gardner, along with Austin-based designer Kimber Reed, formed Reclaimed Space, a firm devoted to small, prefabricated, living spaces. By the beginning of 2011, the firm had constructed six spaces, had lined up another ten, and is out making a name for itself in the world of prefabricated housing.

The focus of Gardner's prefab company is to use reclaimed and repurposed materials as a way of counteracting the amount of energy expended by the building industry, as well as the amount of waste sent to the landfill each year. To source the materials, Gardner and his team post flyers at local events and contact ranchers in person. Often the ranchers are happy that someone wants to take the dilapidated barns and other structures off their property. Sometimes Reclaimed Space has to buy the wood, but usually at a low cost. Their most recent acquisition was the run-down livery that was part of the Shiner Brewery in Shiner, Texas, said to be the oldest structure in the area. Reclaimed Space carefully deconstructed the structure and salvaged every possible item, including a large supply of barn wood and other reclaimable parts, all of which will be used to build several homes.

OPPOSITE
Side entrances to the Land Yacht.

Reclaimed Space's sixth project, the Land Yacht, was built for a couple who are professional yachters and sail around the world most of the year. On their travels, they found a ranch outside of Austin, Texas, and they decided to plant some roots and spend time on solid ground. In a nod to their profession, the one-bedroom house was inspired by the efficient design of a sailboat, including lots of custom-built compartments. A compact kitchen sits inside an open living room; the bedroom and bathroom are on the opposite side of the building. The small yet efficient space also features an attached, screened-in porch, which almost doubles their living space and allows them to take advantage of the warm climate of southeast Texas.

Almost all of the materials for the house are reclaimed or repurposed, and most came from the Shiner livery, including the timbers, planks, wood for the cabinets, and the galvanized tin, which was used for the ceiling and the roof. New materials were used for framing, wiring, fixtures, appliances, and insulation. Passive solar design, large overhangs, and tight, blown-in soy insulation, with R-values of 30 on the roof and 17 in the walls, keep out the heat in summer and retain warmth in winter. A single-pitch shed roof is a low-maintenance design that easily collects rainwater and can support a solar-panel system if the owners ever want to upgrade. Transom windows high on the north wall can be opened to allow for cross ventilation and natural cooling.

Construction of the Land Yacht took eight weeks in Reclaimed Space's factory in Austin. It was then transported by truck to the couple's ranch and installed on a pier foundation. Though all of Reclaimed Space's units are prefabricated, they are certainly not mass produced. The work is handcrafted and custom built to make the best use of the salvaged materials. A crew of extremely talented carpenters and craftsmen is required to build these unique structures. The homes are almost entirely complete when they are ready to leave the factory and need only be placed correctly on a low-impact, concrete pier foundation and connected to utilities. These modular units are transported on the back of tilt-bed trucks and are no wider than your standard eighteen-wheeler, which minimizes shipping costs.

LEFT

The kitchenette.

RIGHT

Interior view into the dining area and kitchen.

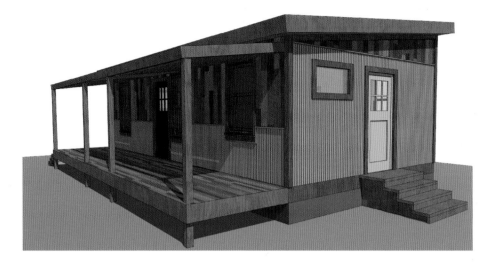

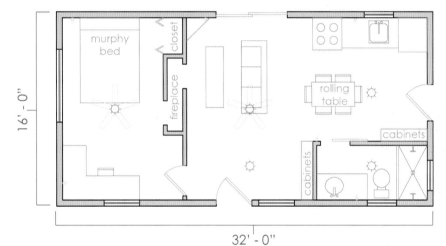

These small spaces promote living mindfully and lightly on the earth and make use of good materials that would otherwise go to waste. By building energy-efficient structures from salvaged materials, Reclaimed Space is reducing the impact of new construction. Each Reclaimed Space house makes use of passive solar design, can easily incorporate renewable energy and rainwater collection, as well as many other sustainable strategies and systems, and can even be designed for off-grid applications. Easily transported, these artistically unique modern and rustic modular homes can be combined in various configurations to create larger structures. At an average cost of $115 per square foot, Reclaimed Space offers a reasonable price point for sustainable and prefabricated construction. Though it takes skilled craftsmen to build these prefab homes, that does not seem to lengthen the construction time, which is reasonably quick. The beauty of these homes lies in the efficient incorporation of otherwise unusable materials to build them.

ABOVE

Renderings and floorplan of a similarly
sized house as the Land Yacht.

PROJECT NAME
Paonia Solargon

LOCATION
Paonia, Colorado, USA

PROJECT TEAM
Solargon Structures
(http://www.solargon-structures.com)

MANUFACTURER
Insulated Component Structures
(http://www.ics-rm.net)

DESIGNER
Rob Galloway

PROJECT YEAR
2010

PROJECT AREA
374 square feet

**APPROXIMATE
COST**
$22,500

PHOTOS: JT Thomas Photgraphy (unless otherwise indicated)

4.2

Paonia Solargon

Octagonal structures built with prefabricated SIP panels make low-cost, energy-efficient homes with a small environmental footprint.

Solargon Structures offer a unique product in the prefab industry. Inspired by the yurt but built with high-performance Structural Insulated Panels (SIPs), the octagonal structures can be erected in one or two days. Their small footprint is also a major selling point for many homeowners who want to decrease their environmental footprint and live simpler lives with less "stuff." Solargon was founded by contractor and designer Rob Galloway, who is a big proponent of living small. His small-footprint cabins were originally based on the concept of living lightly off the land and then evolved into the high-performing, passive solar homes that they are today. Many owners of Solargon Structures houses sought out the cabin-like homes because they live in remote locations, are already off the grid, and need an energy-

efficient dwelling that can be quickly erected and powered with renewable-energy systems.

The company began back in 2004 under Rob Galloway, who originally used the traditional stick-built construction method to build the octagonal homes. Seeking out a more energy-efficient method, he contacted the Fort Collins, Colorado, company Insulated Component Structures (ICS), makers of eco SIPs. The two companies eventually joined and now Solargon Structures is part of ICS, which both designs and manufactures the components for the homes. ICS makes various types and sizes of SIP panels, which are constructed out of two sheets of OSB (oriented strand board) with closed-cell polyurethane spray foam sandwiched in between. SIPs serve

OPPOSITE

This 20 foot Solargon Structure
is located in Paonia, Colorado.

both as insulation and as structural members, making them a complete building system. With an R-value of 7 per inch, the SIP, which come in two thicknesses for the structures, have R-values of 28 or 54, far greater than most homes in the U.S. now have. The panels come precut according to the specifications for the home and complete with installation-ready electrical and plumbing channels.

ICS and Solargon are great believers in designing a home correctly for its site in order to make maximum use of free energy and minimize all other energy needed for the home. They educate and advise their clients based on their own developed method, called ODESA, or "Orientation, Design, Envelope, Systems within, and Alternative Energy."

Orientation: First, the home is properly oriented to take advantage of the sun so that it is heated in winter and shaded in summer. *Design:* Second, windows are oriented to the south to draw in sunlight in winter, and the roof is extended to provide shade in summer. *Envelope:* Third, the envelope of the home (walls, doors, windows, roof, and floor) is made tight and well insulated. *Systems within:* Fourth, after maximizing free energy from the sun and creating a high-performance thermal envelope, the most energy-efficient interior systems (appliances, HVAC equipment, and hot-water heater) are installed. *Alternative Energy:* Finally, after ensuring that the home is as energy efficient as possible, alternative energy systems like photovoltaics and wind turbines are properly sized and installed to generate power.

As of 2011, Solargon offered two different models—20 feet and 30 feet in diameter—with eight walls, eight roof panels, and a dome skylight in the center of the roof. All of the necessary panels to construct the home are packaged in a kit that

RIGHT

Manufacturing of 20 foot Solargon Structure in Fort Collins facility. (Photo courtesy of Doug Kirk for Solargon /ICS SIPs)

can easily be transported by a vehicle as small as a 16-foot trailer. Some customers opt to pick up the materials directly from Fort Collins in their own trucks. Assembly of the 20-foot cabin can be done in one day, while the 30-foot cabin may take two to three days. Usually, the foundation has already been laid by the time the kit arrives. The walls are attached to the foundation, raised, and connected together. Then the roof and

skylight are placed on top. Spray foam is used to help seal the joints and ensure a tight envelope. The homes are installed either by private contractors or by the homeowners themselves, which is a significant cost saving for do-it-yourselfers. After the basic structure is assembled, windows, doors, exterior cladding, roofing, and interior finishes are installed, all according to the wants of the homeowners and at their own cost.

TOP

The home is properly oriented to take advantage of the sun so that in the winter, the home is heated and in the summer, shaded.

ABOVE

Rendering of one bedroom 20 foot Solargan Structure. (Brian Propp, ICS SIPs)

Solargon Structures does not provide the exterior cladding, roofing material, or interior finishes, but does advise customers on their options. For instance, this Paonia, Colorado, home was completed by the owner and a hired carpenter in a little over a month. The owners chose to clad the 20-foot Solargon with cedar shingles and a metal roof and added a bathroom on one side and a redwood deck in front. Interior finishes include locally-sourced wood and forged-steel hooks. Energy-efficient appliances and a propane on-demand hot water heater keep energy use to a minimum. Because of the high-performance envelope and low-energy appliances, electric bills for the small home average $28 a month, plus three gallons of propane for hot water and cooking.

TOP

The octagonal structure is similar in concept to a yurt, but is much more energy efficient.

ABOVE

Passive solar design determines window size and orientation.

Solargon and ICS are currently designing a number of new models with square footprints to add to their line of octagonal homes. The homes will range in size from 118 square feet for the smallest model to 700 square feet for the largest, with costs anywhere from $10,000 to $41,500. Solargons can be used for homes, offices, cabins, schoolrooms, and even hotels.

Customers come to Solargon seeking energy-efficient homes with a small environmental footprint. The company has built some thirty homes in the U.S. and Canada, and all of them have received a home energy rating below 50 on the HERS Index. Many even have ratings in the 30s and 40s, making them much more energy efficient than the standard new home, which has a rating of 100. The small physical footprint encourages the homeowner to live lighter and with a lower impact on the earth. In addition to the eco-attributes of the Solargon, the cost is relatively low, especially compared to most prefab homes, making this option attractive for those seeking a hands-on approach to energy-efficient home construction.

ABOVE
A large skylight in the ceiling draws in ample daylighting.

PROJECT NAME
Casa El Tiemblo

LOCATION
El Tiemblo, Avila Province, Spain

ARCHITECT
James&Mau
(http://www.jamesandmau.com)

CONTRACTOR
Infiniski
(http://www.infiniski.com)

INTERIOR DESIGN
Becara
(http://www.becara.com)

PROJECT YEAR
2010

PROJECT AREA
2,045 square feet

APPROXIMATE COST
$176,554 (€140,000)

PHOTOS: Pablo Sarabia

4.3

Casa El Tiemblo

Four stacked shipping containers create a luxurious, modern, low-cost, and energy-efficient home in central Spain.

"Affordable luxury" may seem like an oxymoron, unless you have Madrid-based architects James&Mau and shipping-container house builders Infiniski on your team. The driving theory behind their work is to find smarter approaches to housing that are cheaper, faster, and more environmentally responsible. Often, the most cost-effective way for them to achieve the results they want is to use recycled materials, like used containers, train rails, shipping pallets, bottles, or recycled aluminum, iron, and wood. With more than ten completed houses in their portfolio now, James&Mau and Infiniski have begun to perfect their prefabrication techniques and are creating a whole new genre of housing in which recycled materials and luxury coexist. One of their latest projects is a modern,

low-cost, and energy-efficient three-bedroom home outside of Madrid, most of which is made from recycled materials.

The client for whom this house was built wanted something different, creative, and modern, but at the same time he didn't have a ton of money to throw at it. Located in El Tiemblo, a small town about an hour and a half outside of Madrid, the site is at an elevation of about 1,100 meters (3,600 feet). Temperatures can drop quite low in the winter but rise quite high in summer, so energy-efficient heating, insulation, and cooling were design priorities for James&Mau, which is led by Jaime Gaztelu González-Camino and Mauricio Galeano Escobar.

OPPOSITE

Four used shipping containers were used to construct this 3 bedroom home.

Four bright blue, 40-foot-long cube containers were bought in the port of Valencia and trucked four hours to a warehouse in Madrid. Most of the alterations to the containers were prefabricated to minimize site work. A concrete foundation with steel plates was poured on site and then the containers were trucked in, lifted onto the foundation, and welded into place. The home is L-shaped, with two containers on the ground floor and two on the second. A light-filled, steel-and-glass structure, which serves as the living, dining, and kitchen area on the ground floor, provides the supports for the two upper containers, where the owner's study, master bedroom, bathroom, and walk-in closet are located. The two containers on the ground floor hold two more bedrooms, a common room, and a bathroom.

TOP

Most of the alterations to the containers were prefabricated in order to minimize site work.

ABOVE LEFT

The master bedroom is located upstairs and is two containers wide.

which encourage cross breezes and natural ventilation. A biomass system provides additional heat during the winter and hot water all year long. Insulation underneath the home is made from cork, a major export of nearby Portugal, and recycled cellulose insulation was blown into the walls and ceilings, which are 8 cm (3 inches) and 12 cm (4¾ inches) thick, respectively.

Infiniski believes that scrap materials can always be reused. When walls were cut out of the containers to combine them, the leftover corrugated metal pieces were used for other parts of the house. For instance, the exterior wall on the ground floor by the front steps was originally part of the containers. Recycled gypsum and cellulose fiberboards were used for the interior walls instead of pure gypsum wallboards, which require a lot of energy to produce. Inside, eco-friendly, low-VOC (volatile organic compounds) paints were used on the walls. The owner was also particularly fond of the original color of the containers, so instead of repainting them completely, patches in need of repair were painted to match the existing bright blue exterior. Materials were locally sourced from the Iberian Peninsula, and most of them were recycled. In fact, 70 percent of the home's materials (measured by weight) were recycled, repurposed, or reused.

Oriented to the south and away from the street, the main room enjoys privacy, views of the mountains and valley, and the sun's light and heat, which is especially important in the winter. To minimize energy usage, passive solar design was utilized so the sun heats the home in the winter, and shade trees were planted specifically to provide shade for the home in the summer when the sun is high. Roll-down shades in the living area protect the space from overheating. There is no air-conditioning system; cooling is generated entirely through operable windows and doors,

TOP LEFT
Custom glass doors were made to fit the space left open by the steel cargo door.

TOP RIGHT
The living room is made from a steel structure the size of two containers and then fitted with large windows.

ABOVE LEFT
All the metal cut out from the containers is used somewhere in the project.

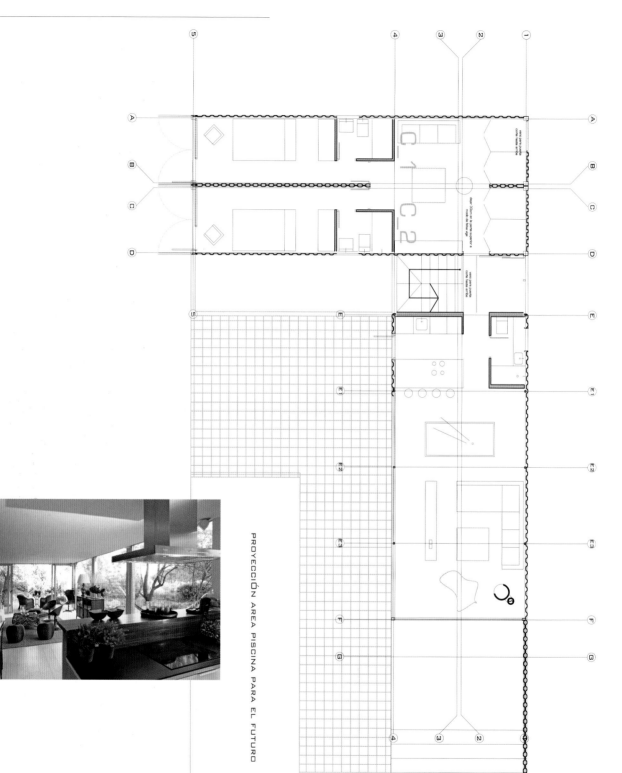

PROYECCIÓN ÁREA PISCINA PARA EL FUTURO

LEFT

A small kitchen opens up into the living room.

RIGHT

Ground floorplan of Casa El Tiemblo.

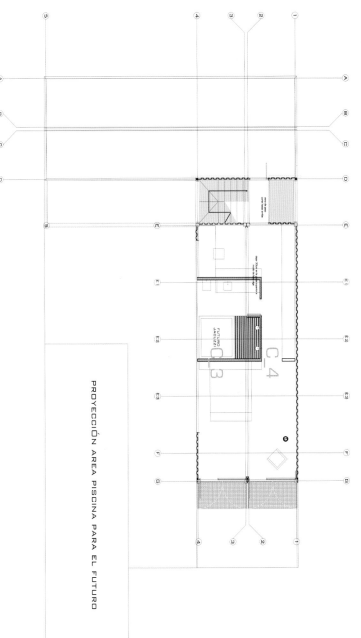

The entire project took six months to finish: three months of prefabrication in the Madrid warehouse and three months on site to place the containers and finish the interior. Overall, the home had a relatively low price point—140,000 euros (around US $190,000), or less than $100 per square foot. Considering the high quality of the construction and the interior finish, it is luxurious housing at a very reasonable price. Shipping-container modular housing can be built quickly and at low cost, certainly an advantage over traditional construction methods.

Infiniski and James&Mau have a number of other projects in progress in both Spain and Chile, which are their main markets, but they hope to be building in other countries soon. Their building process is based on a combination of sustainability, economy, and modernity, all of which are clearly evident in Casa El Tiemblo.

LEFT

First floorplan of Casa El Tiemblo.

RIGHT

Out on the deck, the container ID numbers are still visible on the doors.

PROJECT NAME
Bergwijkpark

LOCATION
Diemen, The Netherlands

PROJECT TEAM
Tempohousing
(http://www.tempohousing.com)

ARCHITECT
DOK Architecten
(http://www.dokarchitecten.nl)

HOUSING MANAGER
Studenten Wonig Web
(http://www.studentenwoningweb.nl)

SITE WORK
SMT Bouw (http://www.smtbouw.nl)

PARTNER ORGANIZATION
De Key Housing
Association, Amsterdam

PROJECT YEAR
2008

PROJECT AREA
81,374 square feet

APPROXIMATE COST
$9,000,000 (€6,788,988)

4.4

Bergwijkpark

Specially designed shipping containers stack to create student housing that can be unplugged and moved to a new site where housing is needed.

A serious lack of student housing in Amsterdam and the surrounding towns forced the area's universities to seek out affordable housing solutions. In May 2006, Tempohousing completed their first student housing project in Amsterdam called Keetwonen, which supplied a thousand housing units to university students. Tempohousing is an Amsterdam-based construction firm with considerable experience designing prefabricated container housing. Built out of recycled shipping containers, the Keetwonen development revolutionized the use of containers for housing on a large-scale basis and is considered the largest shipping-container project in the world to date. In the future, if housing is no longer as scarce in Amsterdam, the entire project could be moved to another location where more housing is needed.

For the Keetwonen project, the containers were stacked five high. Exterior staircases and walkways lead to each container apartment without the support of a superstructure. Six buildings of various sizes were positioned in such a way as to create a protected courtyard with bike parking and private meeting spaces. The project also included an outdoor basketball court, a supermarket, a launderette, a café, and several office spaces, all using the common building block of a 40-foot shipping container. Keetwonen was and still is so popular that even after five years, there is a year and a half waiting list to secure a studio apartment there.

Drawing on the success of Keetwonen, Tempohousing was asked by Hogeschool Inholland and the De Key Housing Association to build another

Student housing project made from
shipping containers in the Netherlands.

student housing project in Diemen, outside of Amsterdam. The university had a strict budget and time limit for construction, so the economics and building time for a container housing project like Keetwonen appealed to them. Hogeschool Inholland had a site for the housing located conveniently close to subway and train stations, as well as to one of the major roads circling the metropolitan area. Compared to Keetwonen's 1,000 studio apartments, Bergwijkpark is much smaller, with only 250 units.

Bergwijkpark is composed of four building blocks surrounding a large courtyard and green space and also includes bike parking, a laundry facility, supermarket, caretaker office, and basketball court. Containers are stacked five units high on top of a concrete foundation. There is no additional structural support or framing for the

TOP
The housing project is composed of four buildings each five stories high.

ABOVE LEFT
The catwalks connect all of the buildings to each other.

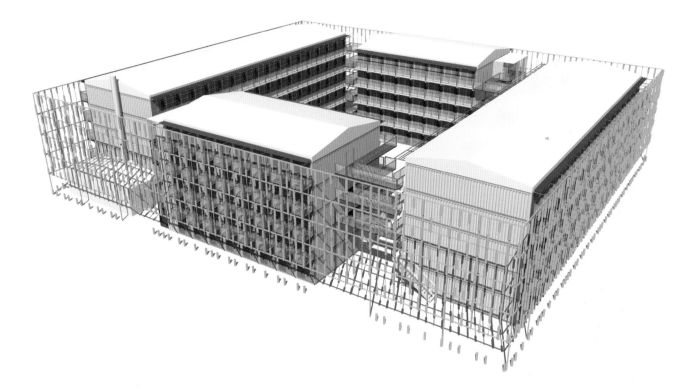

containers. Apartments are accessed by exterior staircases and concrete walkways, which face the courtyard, and each apartment enjoys a private balcony on the exterior side. The roofs were fabricated from steel-framed trusses and insulated panels that were mounted on top of the container blocks.

Tempohousing took much of what they learned from Keetwonen to improve upon their shipping-container housing design. For example, in Bergwijkpark, concrete replaced wood on the walkways to make the units more fireproof, improving the safety rating. Exterior lighting and a decorative, green architectural façade makes the gray container buildings more attractive. Unlike Keetwonen, Bergwijkpark makes use of brand-new containers, specifically designed and built in China for Tempohousing as studio apart-

TOP
Rendering of the Bergwijkpark housing project.

ABOVE LEFT
Exterior stairwell accesses the higher floors.

ments rather than for shipping goods overseas. Though it would be much more sustainable to repurpose used shipping containers, it is likely very cost effective to use new containers specially designed for the purpose.

Each unit is insulated with polyurethane foam and contains its own kitchen, bathroom (shower, toilet, sink), closet, and bedroom area. One large natural gas–fueled boiler in a container on the ground floor provides radiant heating for the entire project, and residents of each unit can control their own temperature and ventilation. Air conditioning is rarely necessary in Holland, so natural ventilation and operable windows provide any cooling that is needed.

Construction of the entire project took hardly any time at all; from start to finish, Tempohous-

TOP
One container on the ground floor holds a large natural gas fired boiler for radiant heating in the apartments.

ABOVE LEFT
Brand-new containers were expressly built in China to serve as studio apartments.

ing completed all 250 housing units in 16 weeks, and cost €6,788,988 (about $9,000,000). The project involved a small amount of site work, consisting of laying the foundation, stacking the containers, adding the roof, and finishing the interior of each apartment. One of the most amazing features of the project is that it could be picked up and moved if the university wanted to change its location. Bergwijkpark was actually designed to be mobile in the event that the university no longer had a need for the residential complex or wanted to relocate or sell it. The containers could simply be unplugged and unstacked in the same manner that they were installed, and then they could be shipped anywhere in the world, just like a standard shipping container. This ability to be mobile gives the housing project a practically infinite life, as there will always be a need for housing somewhere in the world.

In September 2008, Tempohousing also completed a housing project for the Dutch branch of the Salvation Army (Leger des Heils) in

Amsterdam. Similar in design and construction to the Bergwijkpark, the Salvation Army project consists of three-story building blocks with only sixty apartments. In the near future, the firm has plans to build a number of other student housing projects in Amsterdam and hotels around the world. They would like to include solar power and geothermal heat pumps to reduce energy usage, and additional insulation for greater energy efficiency.

TOP LEFT

The bedroom in the back and a small space for storage.

TOP RIGHT

Inside, the apartments are long and narrow with a bathroom the seperates the living space from the bedroom.

ABOVE RIGHT

A unique architectural green façade was included to help make the containers more attractive.

PROJECT NAME
Pioneer Cabin

LOCATION
Golden, British Columbia,
Canada

PROJECT TEAM
Form & Forest
(http://www.formandforest.com)

ARCHITEC
D'Arcy Jones Design
(http://www.darcyjones.com)

ENGINEERING
Wicke Herfst Maver
Structural Engineers

SEPTIC
Peat Moss System
by Ecoflo®

INTERIOR DESIGN
Form & Forest

PROJECT YEAR
2011

PROJECT AREA
1,740 square feet

APPROXIMATE COST
$124,900

PHOTOS: Form & Forest

4.5

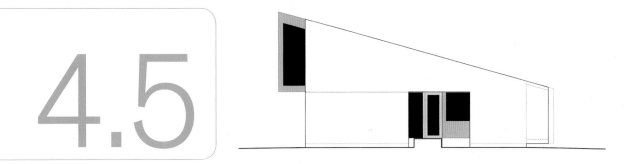

Pioneer Cabin

A prefab kit home shows off its energy-efficient design and gives a new twist to the log cabin in the Canadian Rockies.

Brothers Ryan and Jeff Jordan share a love of the great outdoors and often spend their weekends in the woods of the Canadian Rockies in British Columbia. They decided to take their twin passions for good contemporary design and nature and merge them into a company that could help others get away from it all and enjoy the out-of-doors. Disappointed by the prefab cabin options available on the market, the brothers saw an opportunity to meet a growing demand by offering well-designed, energy-efficient cabins. Inspired by pioneers who lived off the land, in 2008 they started Form & Forest, a company devoted to designing and manufacturing quality prefab cabin kits, which are flat packed at the factory, transported, and assembled on site.

Ryan, who has a background in industrial design, is in charge of the designs, while Jeff, who had run a prefab company for five years, is in charge of the manufacturing. The brothers brought in long-time friend and architect D'Arcy Jones to design the original collection of cabins for the firm. Characterized by simple, clean lines, large picture windows to bring in daylight and nature, and efficient use of space, Form & Forest cabins challenge the notion of what a traditional Canadian cabin should be. Their goals were to create simple homes that require little maintenance and remain durable regardless of the weather conditions throughout the year. At the same time, the cabins had to be beautiful, blend in with the surrounding landscape, and provide a deep connection with nature. Though originally intended for

---

OPPOSITE

Cabins are clad with Hardi Panel, Cedar channel siding and cedar decking, and standing seam metal is used on the mono-pitch roofs.

ABOVE

West Elevation of the Pioneer Cabin.

177

use as vacation retreats in remote locations, the cabins can also fit into an urban environment.

Like many new prefab home builders in the last few years, the Jordan brothers discovered that buyers were few and far between, and with the economy slowly rebounding, they decided that the best way to show off their ideas was to build a model cabin. Their proof of concept was a two-bedroom Pioneer Cabin assembled in eight months on a five-acre plot of land in the wilderness outside of Golden, British Columbia. The living, dining, and kitchen areas enjoy 180 degrees of views through the floor-to-ceiling windows, which let in an abundance of light. A mono-pitch roof, which sheds the heavy snow loads, angles up from the living room to a can-tilevered loft. The home has one bedroom and bathroom in the loft upstairs and another bed-

room and bathroom on the ground floor. Heating is provided by an energy-efficient Morsø wood stove, supplemented by baseboard radiant heaters when necessary. In summer, natural ventilation and cross breezes flowing through operable windows keep the home cool.

All Form & Forest cabins can be easily modified for off-grid situations by adding photovoltaics or solar hot-water heaters on the roof and by collecting rainwater for use inside the house. This particular site had a grid connection, so solar panels were not required, but it was oriented in such a way that the roof could maximize the solar exposure for a future system. There was no sewer connection, so a septic system had to be installed. For this they used an Ecoflo® system, which relies on a sphagnum peat moss filter that retains its purifying capabilities much longer

than conventional systems do. Because it breaks down the wastewater more efficiently, this long-lasting system is far more sustainable for the environment.

Form & Forest cabins are made from prefab kits manufactured in central Alberta. Spruce, pine, and fir wood for the wall and roof panels is sourced from mills in British Columbia and Alberta, with FSC (Forest Stewardship Council)-certified wood mixed in whenever possible. All of the parts, pieces, finish materials, insulation, and appliances are flat packed and shipped overland by truck, or in a cargo container if sent abroad. For the foundation, Insulated Concrete Forms (ICFs) are easily laid by two people like Lego blocks and then filled with concrete. The wall panels are then raised into place, the siding and roofing are added, and finally the windows

are set into place. The cabins are clad in Har-diPanel siding, cedar channel siding, and cedar decking. Standing-seam metal panels are used for the mono-pitch roofs. A detailed binder with instructions, construction documents, and information is provided with every home so that a general contractor or even a good do-it-yourselfer can assemble the home on their own. The Pioneer Cabin should take about six months to build, although this one took eight months due to weather delays. Smaller, single-story cabins can be erected even quicker. The kit costs about $125,000, or about $175 to $250 per square foot.

LEFT

View from the living room to the entrance.

RIGHT

The kitchen is spacious enough for entertaining.

1. Entry
2. Kitchen
3. Living
4. Dining
5. Bath
6. Bedroom
7. Utility Closet
8. Closet
9. Patio
10. Covered Deck
11. Loft
12. Reading Nook
13. Fireplace

Because Form & Forest cabins are designed with remote locations in mind, the prefabricated parts are specifically made for flat packing and easy transport. Bundling all the parts together reduces the impact of transportation and construction. The cabin's tight envelope and high-performance insulation and foundation ensure an energy-efficient home that can easily go off-grid for those who want to live with a lighter impact on the land and a closer connection to nature.

In 2011 Form & Forest was working on completing seven homes in upper Northwest Canada. In the long term, they intend to expand their line

TOP	ABOVE LEFT	ABOVE RIGHT
Floorplan of the Pioneer Cabin.	Looking down from the loft onto the dining table in the living room.	Heating is provided via an energy efficient Morsø wood stove along with baseboard radiant heaters when necessary.

and commission more designers to create new, nature-inspired contemporary cabins. Though now on the higher end of the market, as their commissions increase the firm hopes to bring down costs, improve efficiency, and influence the prefab market. As many people look for a simpler life with a stronger connection to nature, living off the land, and reducing their environmental impact, prefab builders like Form & Forest can provide the means to achieve that goal.

TOP LEFT
The living room enjoys 180 degree views.

TOP RIGHT
The upstairs loft can be used as an extra bedroom.

CENTER RIGHT
A single-pitch roof helps shed snow and is perfectly oriented for a future solar system.

ABOVE RIGHT
The upstairs is cantilevered out to provide more space and to create a covered deck.

PROJECT NAME
Blu Evolution
(http://www.bluhomes.com)

LOCATION
South Lake Tahoe,
California, USA

PROJECT TEAM
Blu Homes
(http://www.bluhomes.com)

PROJECT YEAR
2011

PROJECT AREA
1,560 square feet

APPROXIMATE COST
$340,000

4.6

Blu Evolution

A California family desiring an energy-efficient, sustainable, well-constructed, and low-maintenance vacation home chooses an innovative prefab builder.

When Milli Josifovska and her husband set their hearts on a vacation home in South Lake Tahoe, they knew they wanted an energy-efficient house that required little maintenance. She had in mind a house of the same quality and efficiency as the homes in her native Sweden. The couple looked at existing homes on the market but were disappointed in the quality of construction and didn't want to spend thousands of dollars improving any of them. At the same time, they didn't want to go through the process of building a home from the ground up, as they had done with their primary home in the Bay Area. After a considerable amount of research, the couple decided that going the prefab route was the easiest way to get the home of their dreams with little work on their part and a guarantee of quality construction, energy efficiency, and sustainability.

Josifovska and her husband chose Massachusetts-based Blu Homes to build the turnkey home for their lot in South Lake Tahoe. Taking into account the lot's size and layout, as well as their desire for a four-bedroom home, they determined that of Blu's many home designs, the two-story Evolution would be the best fit. Once they decided on the design, all they had to do was pick out the interior and exterior finishes for fabrication in Blu's Massachusetts factory to begin. Meanwhile, Blu also helped Josifovska arrange permitting and the excavation and pouring of the foundation, all of which was done long before the home was shipped in January 2011.

The entire home was built in the factory by a crew of prefab building experts, who constructed the frame, added insulation, the interior and

OPPOSITE

Blu Homes' four-bedroom Evolution prefab home in South Lake Tahoe, California.

ABOVE

Side cross section of the Blu Evolution.

183

exterior walls, all the interior finishes, and even the appliances. All of the walls came primed and ready for interior paint, and the lighting and plumbing were preinstalled. When the house was ready, the crew folded it up so it could fit on a standard flatbed truck for easier and more cost-effective delivery. This particular house required three trucks to transport the modules and parts across the country. Upon arrival, a crane lifted the three modules off the trucks one at a time, set them into place, and unfolded them. The same crew that built the home in the factory was on hand for the installation to ensure that it was put together correctly on site. It took the set crew less than a day and a half to install the modules and another ten days to completely finish the home. The set crew installed the flooring, hooked up the utilities, inserted the closets, and made sure that all of the parts fit together and operated correctly.

In total, from design until the home was installed and finished, the entire process took ten months, far faster than traditional stick-built home construction. The process was also relatively simple for the homeowner, requiring only that they decide on the floor plan and pick out the finishes from the suggestions that Blu offered. Each Blu home comes standard with radiant floor heating, bamboo floors, an energy-efficient heating and cooling system, low-flow water fixtures, and a combination of rigid foam and EcoBatt insulation. Beyond the standard package, homeowners can choose a variety of upgrades, ranging from interior finishes to rooftop photovoltaic systems, green roofs, rainwater collection systems, and electric car outlets. Blu selects all of the upgrade options based on their eco-friendliness and energy efficiency.

Josifovska chose to upgrade many of her interior finishes to more premium products, like eco-concrete countertops, EcoUrban Veneer cabinets, and Italian glass tile. The exterior of the home is clad in HardiePlank, a fiber cement siding that is very low maintenance, needs to be painted only once, and is fire resistant. Cedar accents, wood-framed, double-paned windows, and a metal roof finish the exterior.

LEFT

RIGHT

One of the two bathrooms.

Blu Homes takes the guesswork out of designing by suggesting eco-friendly materials and finishes.

Though some may take issue with a home that is built so far away from its final location, there are a number of advantages to Blu Homes' prefab process. Fabrication in the factory is resource efficient and little is wasted. Blu also has a very high commitment to energy-efficient homes; on average, Blu's homes are 50–70 percent more energy efficient than the standard home, owing to the supertight envelope construction, thick insulation, and energy-efficient appliances. Blu makes the choice of eco-friendly materials far simpler for clients than most builders, as Blu has researched many materials and suggests only those that are better for the environment and healthier for the home. The company also offers a three-year warranty on the interior of the home and a five-year warranty on the exterior, which ensures that the home will be constructed correctly and last a long time.

Since Blu Homes was founded in 2007, the prefab company has built more than seventy-five homes, including some designed by Michelle Kaufmann, whose firm, mkDesigns, was acquired by Blu in 2010. Blu Homes is expanding its market in the United States and has opened a West Coast manufacturing plant to reduce transportation distances. Energy efficiency is one of the company's top priorities, and they continuously work on improving their designs to make their homes even more efficient.

TOP

A picnic style dining room table accomodates the large family and their guests.

ABOVE RIGHT

Blu Homes are prefabricated in a factory, folded for more compact shipping, and then installed on site.

PROJECT NAME
Lancaster Live/Work
Townhome

LOCATION
Oakland, California,
USA

BUILDER/DEVELOPER
ZETA Communities
(http://www.
ZETAcommunities.com)

ARCHITECT
Daniel Smith & Associates
Architects
(http://www.dsaarch.com)

BUILDING SCIENCES
Building Science Corporation
(http://www.buildingscience.com)

ENGINEERING
Tipping Mar
(http://www.tippingmar.com)

PROJECT YEAR
2009

PROJECT AREA
1,540 square feet

APPROXIMATE COST
$258,000

4.7

Lancaster Live/ Work Townhome

A net-zero energy, urban infill, prefab project in Oakland has a dual purpose, serving as both a home and an office.

For the self-employed professional, renting a separate office is sometimes cost prohibitive. The best solution is to have an office right in one's home, ideally a quiet space separate from the rest of the home. To achieve that may require some remodeling, but in recent years the live/work residence with dedicated space to conduct business has become a popular choice.

The San Francisco–based prefab home manufacturer ZETA Communities has developed just such a live/work townhouse in Oakland, California. The Lancaster Townhome was a prototype home-and-office unit meant for an urban environment. Initially, ZETA intended to build a number of these units in a mixed industrial, artist, and residential neighborhood near the Oakland Estuary. In the end, only the one unit

was completed, but the model proved successful and was well received by the community and the eventual owners. Its exceptionally energy-efficient design, including a rooftop photovoltaic system, makes it a net-zero energy project and earned it a USGBC LEED Platinum certification. The project also garnered a number of other awards and certificates, including a 206 Green Point Rating, the EPA's highest indoor air-quality rating; Indoor airPLUS; the 2009 Green Home Builder of the Year Award; and a 2010 San Francisco AIA design award.

ZETA Communities is both a developer and a prefabricated building manufacturer working in the residential and nonresidential sectors. Originally they developed their own designs and outsourced the fabrication of the modular units,

OPPOSITE

The Lancaster Live/Work townhome in
Oakland has an office downstairs and two
bedroom upstairs. (Nandita Geerdink)

187

but they were disappointed by the manufacturers they tried to work with. As a result, in 2009 the company acquired a 91,000-square-foot manufacturing facility in Sacramento so they could ensure the quality and timeliness of their manufacturing. Unlike most green builders and prefab home manufacturers, ZETA builds only net-zero energy residences and buildings. ZETA's goal with the net-zero energy platform is to challenge traditional building methods, reduce waste, take advantage of urban infill, and make net-zero energy cost effective. They want to build durable, healthy, and energy-efficient buildings for everyone, not just for those with ample funds. ZETA enlisted the consulting services of Daniel Smith & Associates Architects, as well as engineering and building energy experts to design the two-story modular home.

The Lancaster Live/Work Townhome is located in a dense urban environment, close to mass transit, shopping, and services. A zero-lot-line house, it takes full advantage of its plot; the garage and front door come right up to the sidewalk. The ground floor includes a foyer, full bathroom, and a large office area that leads to a small backyard. The main residence upstairs has two bedrooms, a bathroom, and a large, open-plan kitchen, dining, and living space with a private deck. A skylight above the stairwell brightens the space and brings daylight down to the ground floor, and windows at the front and back draw in even more daylight.

Healthy indoor air quality is maintained by a whole-house ventilation system, and operable windows provide natural ventilation. Good air quality is further promoted by the use of low VOC finishes, zero VOC paints, and no formaldehyde, as well as by moisture- and mold-prevention strategies. Environmentally friendly materials like fly ash and cement floors, FSC-certified lumber, artisan ceramic tiles, 100 percent recycled glass, and cement-composite countertops are used throughout. Water-efficient fixtures are coupled with drought-tolerant landscaping to minimize the use of water.

To achieve net-zero energy, it is essential to minimize energy usage within the home, first and foremost by creating a very tight building envelope. Because prefab construction affords the builder a high level of control over the building specifications, ZETA was able to achieve an exceptionally efficient envelope. They used recycled cellulose and spray foam insulation,

TOP
A wood slat sliding door hides the house's trash can.

ABOVE
The office is located on the ground floor in the back and enjoys its own private patio.

TOP LEFT

Craning in a modular unit. (ZETA Communities)

TOP RIGHT

Setting the modular units into place. (ZETA Communities)

ABOVE LEFT

A skylight above the staircase helps daylight reach all the way downstairs into the office.

ABOVE RIGHT

An open floor kitchen makes the space feel much larger.

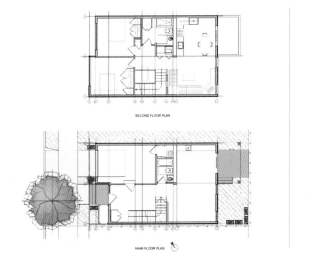

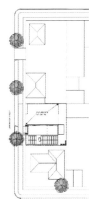

SECOND FLOOR PLAN

MAIN FLOOR PLAN

SITE PLAN

plus rigid foam insulation for an R-30 roof; R-22 walls and floors; and even R-5 and R-7 windows by Serious Materials. All of the systems and appliances are electric, and Energy Star appliances further minimize energy use. This home is gas free and relies solely on the energy supplied by the 5.4 kW rooftop photovoltaic system, thus making it carbon neutral as well. The home requires about 7,850 kW per year and generates about 7,880, ensuring that it always produces more than it uses.

Designing and building a compact home in an urban environment encourages sustainable living and a lower impact on the environment. The

TOP
Floorplans and site plan for Lancaster Live/Work Townhouse. (Dan Smith Architects)

ABOVE LEFT
The open floorplan living room is filled with daylight.

ABOVE RIGHT
Rendering of multiple live/work townhomes in a row. (ZETA Communities)

The Lancaster Live/Work Townhome cost about $165 per square foot. This price included the prefabricated home, zero-energy mechanical package, solar panels, Energy Star appliances, shipping, installation, and on-site finish work, but not the land, site work, or foundation. This is certainly not an "affordable" price in the sense of low-income housing, but in the high-cost Bay Area, it is more affordable than most new construction. ZETA expects to complete a number of truly affordable projects in the next few years.

couple who eventually bought the home after it was completed successfully run their practice from the ground-floor office, thus minimizing their expenses as well as the environmental impact from commuting and maintaining a separate office. Living in a 100 percent electric home powered entirely by a photovoltaic system not only creates a carbon-neutral environment but also proves that it is possible to meet the Department of Energy's goal for all new homes to be cost neutral and net zero energy by 2020. In addition, the couple enjoys paying practically nothing for their energy usage, and as utility costs rise, their savings will only increase.

ZETA Communities is continuing to design and build prefab modular homes and further develop their net-zero energy program with the ultimate goal of making it affordable for everyone.

LEFT
A sunny deck upstairs sits right off the kitchen.

TOP RIGHT
A large work table provides space for client meetings.

PROJECT NAME
BaleHaus@Bath

LOCATION
Bath, UK

PROJECT TEAM
ModCell®
(http://www.modcell.com)

**ARCHITECTURE
AND LANDSCAPE**
White Design
(http://www.white-design.com)

**CIVIL AND
STRUCTURAL DESIGN**
Integral Engineering Design
(http://www.integral-engineering.
co.uk)

ENERGY STRATEGY
ProGETIC
(http://www.progetic.com)

**RESEARCH
ASSISTANCE**
Professor Pete Walker
at the University of Bath

PROJECT YEAR
2009

PROJECT AREA
926 square feet

APPROXIMATE COST
Approximately
$145,354–174,425
(£92,600–111,120)

PHOTOS: ModCell 2011 (unless otherwise indicated)

4.8

BaleHaus@Bath

Straw bales find their way into mainstream construction through prefabrication, resulting in strong, energy-efficient homes.

Straw-bale construction is typically viewed as a craft, as it requires skill, knowledge, experience, and an artist's touch. Almost everything that goes into a straw-bale home is handmade and can be labor intensive, and though the materials are not usually expensive, the labor costs add up quickly. The construction method may not be known for its speed or replication on a large scale, but it is known for its high insulation values and energy-efficient design. As straw is so easily sourced almost anywhere in the world, it makes sense to use it for building insulation, but straw bales have mostly been used for one-off projects. About a decade ago, UK prefab builder Mod-Cell® set out to prove that straw bales could be used on a much larger scale in modern buildings.

Working with the University of the West of England School of Planning and Architecture, Mod-Cell® built their first prefabricated panels with straw. They constructed a strong wooden frame and then shaped the straw bales to fit into it. A coating of lime render keeps the straw in and allows the panel to breathe so it doesn't retain any moisture. Prefabricating the straw frame also helps avoid straw settlement, a common problem of straw-bale homes. Typically, when straw settles after construction, the structure's strength and energy efficiency can change, but because the straw is pre-compressed in the panels, settlement is not a problem. The frames also make the structure more sound, because they bear the load instead of the straw bales alone.

OPPOSITE

BaleHaus@Bath is a prefabricated straw bale home.

In 2009, ModCell® built their first home using the prefab straw-bale frame technique, the BaleHaus@Bath. The cube-shaped building is designed as a two-bedroom, one-bathroom home, with the living and dining room downstairs and the bedrooms upstairs. BaleHaus@Bath was built collaboratively by ModCell® and the University of Bath to study and research the performance of the straw-bale home. With over three years of performance data linked to weather data taken at fifteen-minute intervals, the researchers now have a great understanding of how straw bale performs. The results of this ongoing study are being used to refine the BaleHaus system and improve performance.

Construction of the BaleHaus prefab straw-bale system relies on engineered frames that are built in the UK according to specifications for the home's design. To minimize transportation costs and embodied energy, ModCell® panels are made within ten miles of the construction site in temporary factories called "Flying Factories." The prefabricated wooden frames are flat packed along with the ingredients for the lime render and shipped to the Flying Factory, where local workers use local straw to complete fabrication of the straw-bale panels. Lime render coats the exterior to keep the straw inside the panel and to provide a breathable exterior. The finished panels are transported the short distance to the home's site and in a matter of days the home is assembled. Conduits inside the panels provide channels for electricity and plumbing, and windows are inserted into pre-framed spaces. Local contractors then put the finishing touches on the house, in accordance

TOP LEFT
BaleHaus@Bath is used by the university for meeting space and offices.

BOTTOM LEFT
The window sills show how thick the straw bale walls are.

TOP RIGHT
The sunny upstairs is large enough for two bedrooms and a bath, but serves as a meeting room right now.

with the design preferences of the owner. Construction of the BaleHaus@Bath took three weeks in the Flying Factory, two and a half days to erect on site, and six weeks to finish the interior.

ModCell®'s straw-bale prefab construction method is an efficient and effective marriage between prefab and traditional straw-bale construction. Prefabrication of the panels allows for consistent quality and greater structural integrity than regular straw-bale construction. The lime render coating on the panels helps regulate the straw bales' moisture content with regard to both the internal and external environment, which creates a healthy environment, reduces the risk of condensation, and eliminates the need for vapor barriers. ModCell®'s panels have insulation R-values of 44 and a high level of airtightness, both of which reduce the need for heating and cooling. ModCell® has also performed simulated wind load testing on the BaleHaus at the level of hurricane-force winds, and the home withstood the forces and exceeded expectations. Constructed almost completely from renewable materials like wood, straw, and hemp, the BaleHaus has a very low carbon footprint. The use of local construction and materials reduces transportation significantly, lowering the environmental impact even further.

TOP LEFT
Straw bales are compressed into a strong wood frame.

TOP CENTER
A coating of lime render keeps the straw in and allows the panel to breath so it doesn't retain any moisture.

TOP RIGHT
The lime render is smoothed to leave a clean finish.

ABOVE LEFT
Large floor to ceiling windows let in a ton of natural daylight.

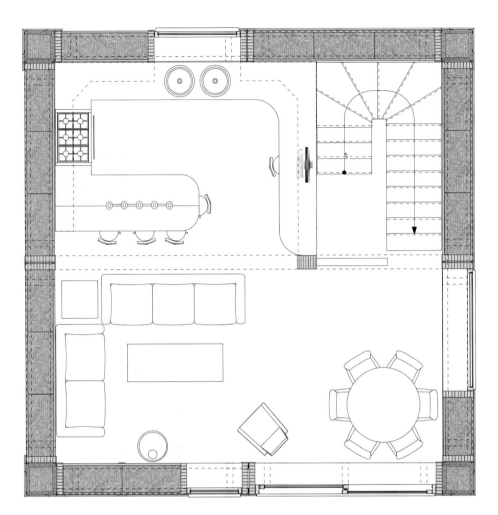

ModCell® is currently working on a twenty-house BaleHaus project in Leeds for LILAC Cohousing Group and has also released designs for prefab straw-bale schools and retail buildings. BaleHaus@Bath will remain at the University of Bath for testing purposes and provides meeting rooms and office space. With a new office in San Francisco, the company plans to expand their reach into the U.S. and demonstrate that their straw-bale prefab construction method is viable, structurally sound, and scalable for the mainstream market.

ABOVE

Ground floorplan of the BaleHaus@Bath.

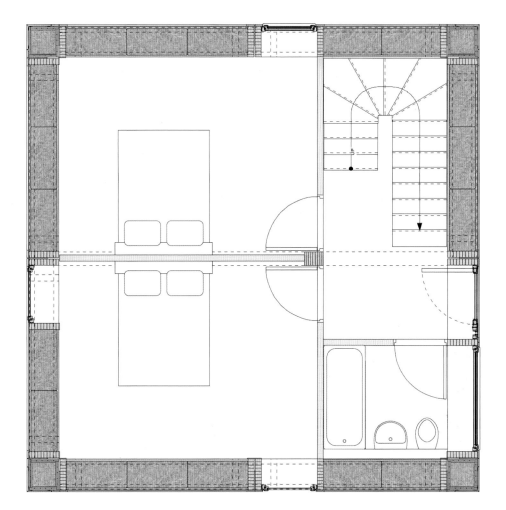

TOP

First floorplan of the BaleHaus@Bath.

ABOVE LEFT

The university is running tests on the home to see how it performs over time.

ABOVE RIGHT

An infrared gun measures where heat is escaping, and since most of the home is blue except for the windows, it means the home is very tight. (Infrared Vision)

5.
ADAPTABLE HOUSING

Homes that are designed and built with the express purpose of dealing with changes to our climate.

As our climate changes so must we, but an even better way of dealing with the future is to prepare for it. Adaptable homes are those that are designed to handle the changes we will face because of climate change—higher temperatures, altered weather patterns, floods, droughts, stronger storms, and so forth. In addition, as we continue to burn through our oil and natural gas resources, we will need to source our energy from more renewable sources. As we will have no choice but to change our ways, why not plan for the future now and save ourselves a lot of trouble and money by building homes that are prepared for climate change? This entails building and adapting our homes to minimize energy use, maximize the conservation of water, minimize waste, use renewable energy systems, and be resistant to future natural disasters.

Adaptable homes are not homes of the future. There already are many homes that make use of existing sustainable technologies and construction techniques, and are equipped to deal with the changes. A given region's climate and disaster risk must be taken into consideration, and governments should adjust building codes in anticipation of the inevitable. With smart and appropriate design, adaptable housing can be constructed at the same cost as traditional construction. Design and construction of adaptable housing should take into account the following elements:

1. **MATERIALS:** Regionally appropriate and locally available materials used in an efficient manner are more sustainable.

2. **ENERGY EFFICIENCY:** Reducing energy use is key to minimizing overall cost and lowering impact on the environment. This will help protect us during heat waves or cold spells, which are likely to occur due to climate change.

3. **WATER EFFICIENCY:** Water is our most precious, most limited resource, so homes must maximize it through rainwater collection, conservation, low-flow faucets, and recycling.

4. **SELF-SUFFICIENCY:** Homes should aim to source their own energy and water, process their own waste, and provide their own food in order to be totally self-sufficient.

5. **DISASTER RESISTANCE:** Homes should be durable and designed to withstand earthquakes, flooding, severe storms, and any other type of natural disaster possible for the region.

This section takes a look at a number of different homes specifically designed to withstand natural disasters typical of their area as well as provide for the residents in a more sustainable manner. All homes, regardless of their location, should be built strong enough to withstand earthquakes and be durable enough to last a century, if not longer. Sustainable design is our best line of defense against climate change, and by investing in our homes and ourselves now, we can reduce costs, damage, and destruction from events in the future.

PROJECT NAME
LIFT House
(http://www.lifthouse.org)

LOCATION
Dhaka, Bangladesh

ARCHITECT
Prithula Prosun

ADVISOR
Dr. Elizabeth English

ENGINEERING AND CONSTRUCTION
ABC Real Estates

CONSTRUCTION SUPERVISION
HBRI (Housing and Building Research Institute) in Bangladesh (http://www.hbri.gov.bd)

CONSTRUCTION
Support Bangladesh Housing and Public Works Ministry and Mr. Mannan Khan

PROJECT YEAR
2010

PROJECT AREA
800 square feet

APPROXIMATE COST
$10,000

PHOTOS: Prithula Prosun

5.1

LIFT House

Designed for the urban poor of Bangladesh, the LIFT House is a safe home that rises and falls with floodwaters and provides the necessary water, electricity, and sanitation for two families.

Dhaka, the capital of Bangladesh, is one of the fastest-growing cities in the world and also one of the poorest. Situated in the floodplains of multiple rivers and subject to monsoons, the city is often inundated with water. As the population continues to grow, the poor are forced into slums, which are often located at low points of elevation and are the worst hit by severe flooding. Dhaka is lacking in adequate infrastructure for electricity, potable water, and sanitation, and conditions only worsen when severe floods occur, leaving the poor helpless against the rising waters. Climate change, rising sea levels, and population growth will only exacerbate the issues in the floodplains of Dhaka and surrounding areas. Low-cost and flood-resilient housing is sorely needed for the urban poor, as well as a more sustainable solution for power, water, and sanitation.

In 2009, Prithula Prosun, originally from Bangladesh, was working to complete her master's degree in architecture at the University of Waterloo in Ontario, Canada. She decided to focus her master's thesis on appropriate architecture for the urban poor of Bangladesh as a way to give something back to her birthplace. As a result, Prosun designed the LIFT House, which stands for Low Income Flood-proof Technology and is an innovative solution for sustainable, flood-resilient housing for low-income communities. The amphibious home does not restrict the flow of rising floodwaters, but instead adapts to the situation by rising with the water, keeping the residents and their possessions dry. Not only is the home designed to survive through flooding, but it is also self-sufficient, providing all the necessary water,

electricity, and sanitation a family might need so they don't have to rely on the city's infra-structure, which often fails.

The amphibious home is a two-story building made up of a solid brick service core with two bamboo structures on either side built upon floating foundations. When floodwaters reach the house, each side of the building rises up on its own floating foundation, guided by a sliding vertical system of steel pipes. Prosun designed and tested two floating foundations, one made out of a lightweight and buoyant ferrocement and the other out of 8,000 reused water bottles collected from the nearby Westin Hotel. Both foundations proved to be successful and applicable in terms of available low-cost materials and the skill level needed to fabricate them.

Constructed out of bamboo, each side of the building serves as a home for a family of five and includes two floors of living and sleeping space. Bamboo was chosen for its local availability,

low cost, and strength. The central service core is built out of brick and reinforced concrete and houses two composting toilets, large water storage tanks, a kitchen for each household, and a shared deck. This deck is accessed via the second floor of the living quarters and becomes usable and safe outdoor space during a flood.

A thatchlike roof, made of bamboo skins, collects rainwater and directs it through a filter into a cistern in the service spine. Collected rainwater is used for bathing, cooking, and washing; drinking water is boiled. Used water from these activities is directed through a biosand filter into a second cistern. This greywater can then be used for toilets or irrigation. Enough clean water can be stored in these two cisterns to last each family through the dry season and through the floods of the rainy season.

LEFT
A rendering showing how the house would rise in flood waters.

RIGHT
A women and her two children sit in the upstairs room.

Access to Bangladesh's urban sewage system is very limited and during severe floods it can become unsafe, get backed up, and spread disease. For the LIFT House, Prosun designed a dual-pit latrine system for each family to ensure that sewage is safely and hygienically contained even during a flood and that waste is eventually used as fertilizer for the families' gardens. Urine is diverted from the solid waste and directed via an underground pipe to fertilize the gardens. Each pit is large enough for five and a half years' worth of solid waste; when it is full, the family closes it off and opens up the second pit. After another five and a half years, the solid waste in the first pit has decomposed into rich manure for the garden.

The LIFT House is also equipped with two 60 kW solar panels on the roof and two batteries, which generate enough power to run several energy-efficient light bulbs and charge cell phones. The solar panels, the water storage, and the composting toilets make the building completely off grid and totally self-sufficient. During a flood, the families do not need to rely on the city for services, utilities, or any aid, and they can live safely on the second floor of their home. The resilient home does not work to resist the forces of the flood and will not be destroyed by them; rather, it floats upon the rising waters and sinks safely to the ground once they have receded. Additionally, low-skilled workers can easily construct the home out of low-cost, renewable materials readily sourced from within or near the city.

In November 2009, Prosun began construction of the LIFT House pilot project at the Housing and Building Research Institute in Dhaka. The project was funded by the IDRC (International Development Research Centre) through the ECOPOLIS

TOP LEFT
The structural frame for the bamboo house.

ABOVE LEFT
A steep bamboo staircase leading downstairs.

TOP RIGHT
Workers installing the bamboo poles onto the vertical steel pipes, which serve as guides when the home rises.

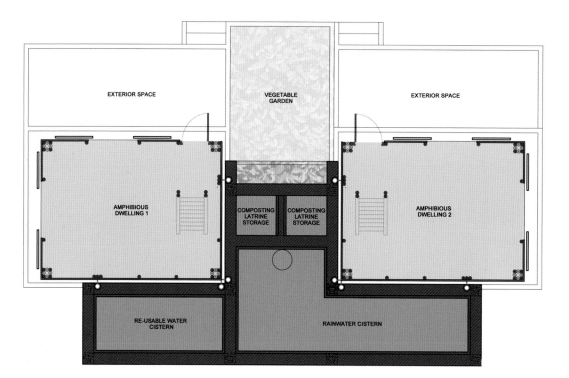

Interior Space of amphibious dwelling

Interior Spaces of the Service Spine

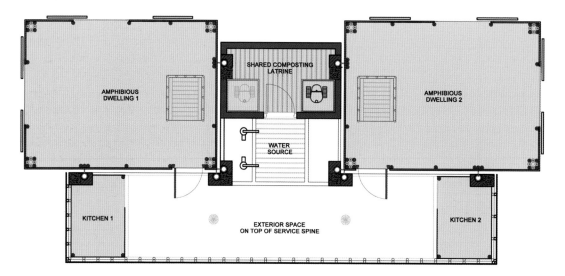

Interior Space of amphibious dwellings, kitchens and shared latrine

TOP

Ground floorplan of the LIFT House.

ABOVE

First floorplan of the LIFT House.

Graduate Research and Design Award. At the end of January 2010, the project was completed and successfully tested by simulating a flood to float the amphibious dwellings. The prototype cost roughly $5,000 for each side, but Prosun anticipates that it will cost much less when the LIFT House is built on a larger scale. Prosun is continuing with her research of amphibious housing and hopes to implement more projects like this in Bangladesh. Currently, a low-income family of five occupies one side of the duplex and the other side is open for tours and demonstrations.

Floods are very much a part of normal life in Bangladesh, but as climate change marches onward, flooding will become much more aggressive and frequent. Low-cost dwellings like the LIFT House are a necessary part of the solution to provide safe housing for the urban poor. The self-sufficient home is sustainable and also allows the residents to maintain a sense of normalcy even during severe floods.

ABOVE
Time lapse photos of the
LIFT House during construction.

PROJECT NAME
Malibu Studio

LOCATION
Malibu, California, USA

PROJECT TEAM
Cory Buckner and
Nick Roberts, AIA
(http://www.corybuckner.com)

OWNER/CLIENT
Cory Buckner and
Nick Roberts

PROJECT YEAR
2009

PROJECT AREA
700 square feet

APPROXIMATE COST
$210,000

PHOTOS: Nick Roberts (unless otherwise indicated)

5.2

Malibu Studio

Located in the Santa Monica Mountains, this weekend studio is specifically built to be fireproof and low impact.

Brush fires in the Santa Monica Mountains outside of Malibu in Southern California are about as common as hurricanes in the Gulf of Mexico. Almost every home in the hills has either been destroyed by fire or had a very close call. Yet despite the ongoing risk, people still want to have homes in the hills with views of the Pacific Ocean and take advantage of the moderate, usually sunny weather. As climate change accelerates, however, temperatures are predicted to rise and in some areas rainfall could go down, increasing the fire danger.

In 1993, Cory Buckner and her husband, Nick Roberts, both architects in the LA area, lost their home to a large brush fire. The house was located on a steeply sloping site, with views of the ocean and Boney Ridge, the highest peak in

the Santa Monica Mountains. The fire danger in the area is extreme; for their site specifically, the danger comes from wind-driven flames on the north and west. After rebuilding their home and learning about the pathways and mechanisms of brush fire, the couple decided to build a weekend retreat that would be completely fireproof, so they could be sure it would not succumb when the next fire rolled up their canyon.

In addition to ensuring fire safety, Buckner and Roberts wanted to build a home that required little energy to stay comfortable, fit in with the context of the natural surroundings, and made use of environmentally friendly materials. They set about designing a small live/work studio house that was restricted in size by the local fire department to less than 700 square feet. Limit-

OPPOSITE

Malibu Studio is a fire proof home in the Santa Monica
Mountains. (www.millerhallphoto.com)

209

ing the footprint of the home forced the couple to get creative with their space and include only what was necessary. Like an inverted pyramid, the walls spread out as they ascend, creating a sense of openness and space despite the small square footage. A double-height ceiling gives the living area a feeling of luxury; the loft bedroom is stacked on top of the laundry and bathroom; and a small office area provides the couple with a workspace.

When building a fireproof home, the first step is to create a defensible space around the house by clearing out most of the vegetation within thirty feet so there is nothing that can serve as fuel. Only close-cropped native grass and fire-tolerant plants are allowed to grow in that space. As winds and fire attack the site from the north, the couple tucked the building back and down into the east hillside, leaving only three sides exposed. The north façade is heavily fortified with Rheinzink, a fire-resistant, fully recyclable zinc alloy with traces of copper and titanium, and the windows are recessed into the armored shell for protection. The best views of the ocean are to the west, so the west façade has large windows that can be covered with metal screens for protection from both fire and the hot afternoon sun. The south façade is completely transparent to let in sunshine and views. Large overhangs above the south façade shade the interior from the sun in the summer but let it in during the winter for passive heating. In theory, the tough, fire-resistant north wall, which also wraps over the roof, can protect the home from any fire danger, but if all else fails, a fire-sprinkler system with two on-site water storage tanks would douse the flames.

TOP
Vegetation surrounding the home was cleared away to create defensible space.

ABOVE
Sliding windows open the interior up to the outdoors to expand the living space.

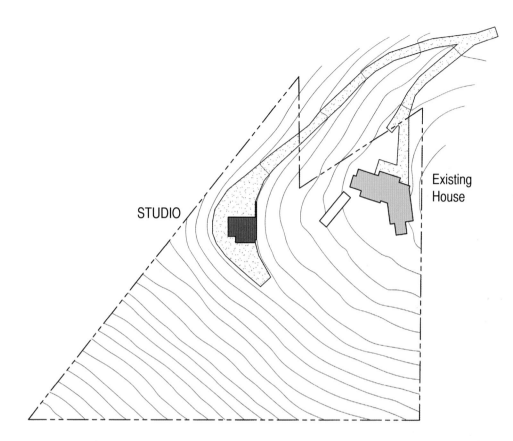

STUDIO

Existing
House

Concrete construction, using 30 percent fly ash, aids the home's passive solar design and acts as thermal mass, soaking up the sun's heat and transferring it to other parts of the house. Ther-mal mass combined with the earth-sheltered design keeps the interior temperature stable. In the winter, when necessary, a tiny propane boiler and radiator system combined with a wood stove provides heat. Most of the time, though, the home needs to shed heat, which is accomplished through natural ventilation from the operable sliding glass doors on the south and a thermal chimney that lets the hot air escape out of the top. Low-E, double-paned windows throughout minimize solar heat gain. Energy-efficient lighting via LEDs helps keep the overall energy usage in the studio very low. The home is still attached to the electric grid, but when funds become available, the entire home will easily run off photovoltaic panels and a solar hot-water system.

TOP
Site plan of Malibu Studio.
(Drawing by Artur Grochowski)

ABOVE
Sliding shades protect the home
against fire and also the hot afternoon
sun. (www.millerhallphoto.com)

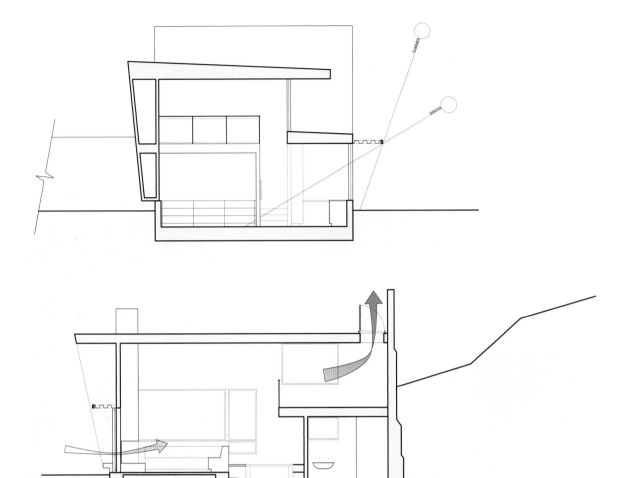

Buckner and Roberts made sure to incorporate low-impact and non-toxic materials into both the interior and the exterior. Walls were covered with low-VOC oriented strand board, which is made from postindustrial wood waste, and engineered lumber beams also help reduce the use of virgin lumber. Concrete, bamboo, and porcelain tile with recycled ceramic content were used as flooring materials. The entire home was heavily insulated with a tight thermal envelope and performs 35 percent better than California's Title 24 building code requires.

The small home is solidly built into the hill and does an admirable job of minimizing the impact on its environment. Camouflaged to match the surrounding chaparral, it is barely visible from across the canyon. Tucked into the hillside and down into the ground, the studio has a low profile, which, along with its fire-resistant design and materials, should enable it to survive when the next fire attacks.

TOP

Solar passive design scheme: Low-angled winter sun streams in through the windows to heat the home, while the summer sun is blocked with shading.

Natural ventilation scheme: Excess heat is shed through natural ventilation, with hot air being sucked up and out of the chimney. (Drawing by Artur Grochowski)

TOP LEFT

The kitchen, bath and dining area is sunk into the hill and sits lower than the living area. (www.millerhallphoto.com)

TOP RIGHT

Built in seating next to a coxy fire enjoys amazing views of the surrounding mountains. (www.millerhallphoto.com)

ABOVE

The studio is neatly designed to fit in with the surrounding environment rather than stand out.

PROJECT NAME
Watervilla "IJburg"

PROJECT TEAM
Waterstudio.NL
(http://waterstudio.nl)

PROJECT AREA
1,883 square feet

LOCATION
IJburg, Amsterdam,
The Netherlands

PROJECT YEAR
2008

APPROXIMATE COST
$390,000

5.3

Watervilla "IJburg"

A floating home in Amsterdam takes advantage of the water-based site, easily adapting to fluctuations in water levels.

The people of The Netherlands and all along the North Sea coast have been working to fight back the rising and falling of the tides with dykes and pumps for thousands of years. As the sea level rises from climate change, holding back the tides will become even more challenging. So rather than fighting the water, why not adapt and learn to live with it? Floating homes provide a surprisingly simple alternative to living on land, and in densely populated Amsterdam, sometimes the water is the only available place to build. Technology and experience have improved considerably in recent years, making the construction of sturdy, stable floating homes possible, so that living on the water is not very different from living on the land.

Dutch architecture firm Waterstudio.NL has been designing and building water-based structures for more than a decade and has over a hundred floating homes under their belt. These water architects envision a future in which urban environments expand out onto the water as a way to cope with the changing climate and to provide more housing for our ever-growing population. One of their more recent floating homes is the Watervilla "IJburg" on the eastern outskirts of Amsterdam. The clients wanted to be able to travel into the city via the waterways, so living on the water made a lot of sense for them.

Floating houses remain buoyant just like a ship or a boat—the weight of the house pushing down on the water is equal to the weight of the water displaced. As long as that balance is maintained, it will float. Watervilla "IJburg" is a three-story

OPPOSITE
Watervilla 'IJburg' sits at the end of a long pier.

the home is cornered by other watervillas. To afford the clients privacy from their neighbors and views of the water beyond, the side facing the other watervillas is solid white stucco with no windows. It features an inscription that reads *cum grege non gradior . . .*, which roughly translates to "I do not walk with the flock." The inscription is both the name of the floating house, just like a boat that has been christened, and a reference to the clients' desire for a somewhat unconventional lifestyle on the water.

Inside, the lowest floor, which is partially below the water level, holds three bedrooms and a bathroom. The ground floor is accessed directly from the pier and contains a bathroom, storage space, and an open-plan living and kitchen area with large sliding glass doors that lead to an attachable deck. A neatly designed cabinet stores the television and other items out of sight. The ceiling is covered in the same wood as that used on the exterior to carry the concept through from the outside to the inside. Two sets of stairs along the back wall access the bedrooms below and the work area and open-air deck above.

home with a square concrete foundation designed so that only the lower portion of the lowest level is underwater. Regardless of whether the water rises or falls, the home will float at the same level and remain stable. The house was constructed in Lelystad, forty miles from Amsterdam, over a seven-month period and when it was finished, it was towed over the water to IJburg.

The home's steel superstructure is covered with white stucco, wood, and floor-to-ceiling glass on three sides. Located at the end of a long pier,

---

TOP LEFT

The first floor contains a work area and an open deck.

ABOVE LEFT

The ground floor is a large open space with a kitchen tucked against the wall and storage and the entertainment center hidden away.

TOP RIGHT

The home was prefabricated and then tugged to its final home on the eastern outskirts of Amsterdam.

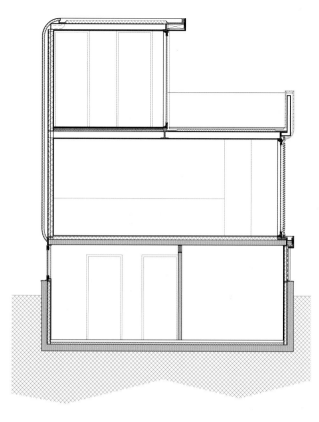

New house construction in Amsterdam is subject to strict energy-efficiency regulations, so this watervilla includes high-efficiency insulation and a tight envelope. A closed-loop ground source heat pump makes use of the relatively constant water temperature below the house to generate energy-efficient heating and cooling. There is also a solar hot-water heating system on the roof to provide domestic hot water. Flexible connections from the pier can attach the watervilla to grid sewage, water, electricity, and gas.

Floating homes are exceptionally versatile and are likely to play a much larger role in housing in the future years. As cities become ever more crowded and dense, development may have no choice but to expand onto the open water. Floating buildings are not permanently fixed and can be relocated, which increases their longevity. Should conditions change in one location, the homes can be towed by water to someplace safer or more desirable. Additionally, floating buildings are flood-proof. As long as the structures are located in a sheltered location, floodwaters will not cause damage, regardless of the tides or sea level. As sea levels continue to rise, floating buildings may become a necessity, especially for countries like the Maldives, which may be completely submerged in the near future.

Waterstudio.NL is on the cutting edge of water-based architecture, designing floating homes, developments, and even master plans for entire water-based neighborhoods and cities. These floating developments would look and feel very much like their land-based counterparts, but would rest on a large floating foundation and successfully and sustainably cope with the fluctuations of our oceans.

LEFT

Cross section of Watervilla "IJburg."

RIGHT

An outdoor deck expands the living space outdoors.

PROJECT NAME
Porchdog House

LOCATION
Biloxi, Mississippi, USA

ARCHITECT
Marlon Blackwell Architect
(http://www.marlonblackwell.com)

PARTNER ORGANIZATIONS
Architecture for Humanity
and the Biloxi Model Home Project
(http://architectureforhumanity.
org/projects/biloxi_model_homes)

GENERAL CONTRACTOR
Holder Construction Company

STRUCTURAL ENGINEERING
Tatum-Smith Engineers, Inc.

STRUCTURAL CONSULTANTS
Black Rock Engineering

PROJECT YEAR
2009

PROJECT AREA
1,525 square feet

APPROXIMATE COST
$197,000

PHOTOS: Timothy Hursely (unless otherwise indicated)

5.4

Porchdog House

The Porchdog House was designed to withstand hurricanes and flooding to ensure that after the next storm, the house will still be there.

Architecture For Humanity asked fifteen firms to design homes to help rebuild the flooded coastal regions of Biloxi after Hurricane Katrina devastated the city. One of the firms that participated and eventually built a home was Marlon Blackwell Architect of Fayetteville, Arkansas. As part of the Biloxi Model Home Project, seven families whose homes were destroyed were given the chance to choose a design and work directly with an architecture firm to rebuild their home on their property. Richard Tyler, a local house-painter and a single father with young children, chose Marlon Blackwell Architect's Porchdog House, a home designed to withstand storm surges and hurricane force winds, with features providing the social qualities of the shotgun-style southern home typical of the area.

Biloxi, Mississippi, is located on a peninsula in the Gulf of Mexico and was hit particularly hard by the hurricane in 2005. A nine-meter storm surge, strong winds, and heavy rain completely inundated the coastal town.[1] During reconstruction, FEMA recommended that all homes be built six to twelve feet above street level to minimize damage from flooding, but building that high off the ground challenges the traditional notion of a streetscape and the porch culture of the South.

In his design for the Porchdog House, Blackwell's focus was on using durable, low-maintenance materials, maximizing the capability of weathering extreme storms, and providing space for social interaction. He also had to comply with the new building regulations for flood-prone areas and raise the house at least six feet off the

OPPOSITE

The Porchdog House retains essential elements of southern living including a large street level porch, but is built off the ground to withstand storm surges.

ground. The typical approach has been to build a shotgun house and place it on stilts, but Blackwell didn't want to compromise the social fabric of the city. He opted instead to place the main living spaces above the flood level but still provide a house front and porch area at street level.

The main living spaces are located on the first and second levels of the three-story home, while the ground level provides covered parking for two cars, storage, and a stoop that serves as a covered porch. A living area, dining room, and kitchen, as well as a bonus room that could serve as an office or an extra bedroom, are located on the first level. The second level contains two bedrooms, a bathroom, and a study. Blackwell designed the interior with plenty of built-in storage and flexible space so the homeowners could furnish and decorate as they chose. A secure deck off the dining room serves as a second porch and an extension of the living space into the outdoors. An industrial roll-up, garage-style door can be lowered over the porch to provide shade, security, or protection against storms.

Structurally, the home is strong and solidly anchored into the ground's mushy soil with a thick, foundation that also acts as a counterweight against uplift. Sheer walls and steel

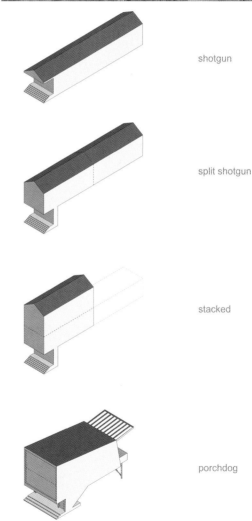

shotgun

split shotgun

stacked

porchdog

TOP LEFT
The Porchdog House is built so that all the critical living spaces are built above the 9-foot water mark.

TOP RIGHT
At the street level, the home maintains an active presence with a covered porch.

ABOVE
Evolution from the traditional shotgun style house to the Porchdog. (Marlon Blackwell Architect)

1 SLIDING PERFORATED
   METAL SCREENS
2 WINDOWS
3 METAL SHELL
4 ROL UP PERFORATED
   METAL SCREENS AND
   SUPPORT STRUCTURE
5 STEEL FRAME
6 METAL SOFFIT
7 CMU BALLAST
   VOLUME
8 FOUNDATIONS
9 PILES

moment frames will help the home resist Category 4 surges and winds. The staircase from the ground to the first level is open to the street; in case of flooding, it will reduce the likelihood of water rushing up into the house. A masonry-block storage area for noncritical supplies and personal items on the ground floor acts as ballast against strong wind and water forces. Finally, metal shutters on the east façade and the roll-up door on the porch can be locked down with padlocks in the event of a storm or for extra security.

Materials were chosen for their durability and low maintenance, keeping in mind how poorly most homes are actually maintained. For instance, the exterior is clad in a ribbed-metal skin; powder coated in white, it should never need to be repainted. The steel used as the framing material and for the porch will need minimal

LEFT

Exploded view of the components of the Porchdog House. (Marlon Blackwell Architect)

RIGHT

An open floorplan living and kitchen area provides a large communal spot for the family.

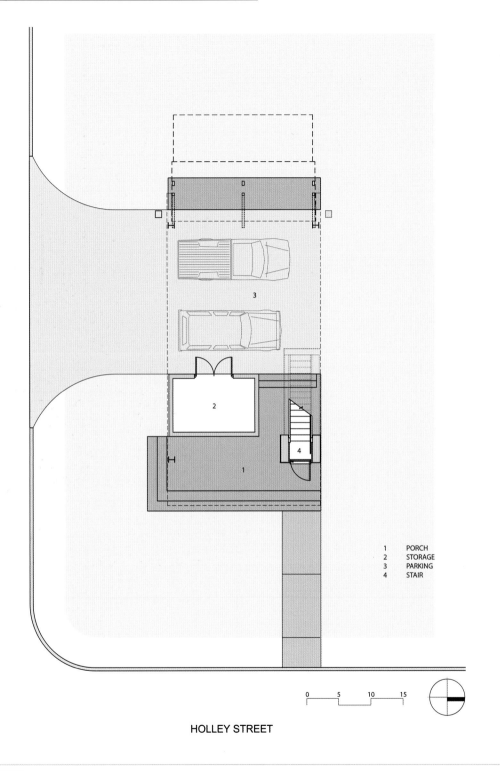

AUSTIN STREET

1   PORCH
2   STORAGE
3   PARKING
4   STAIR

0   5   10   15

HOLLEY STREET

ABOVE

Ground floorplan of the Porchdog
House. (Marlon Blackwell Architect)

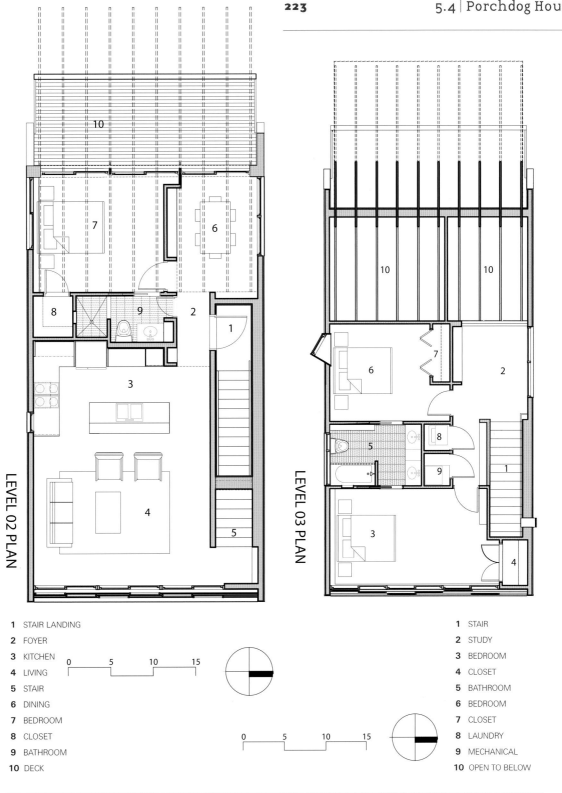

LEVEL 02 PLAN

LEVEL 03 PLAN

1	STAIR LANDING
2	FOYER
3	KITCHEN
4	LIVING
5	STAIR
6	DINING
7	BEDROOM
8	CLOSET
9	BATHROOM
10	DECK

0   5   10   15

1	STAIR
2	STUDY
3	BEDROOM
4	CLOSET
5	BATHROOM
6	BEDROOM
7	CLOSET
8	LAUNDRY
9	MECHANICAL
10	OPEN TO BELOW

0   5   10   15

LEFT

First floorplan of the Porchdog House. (Marlon Blackwell Architect)

RIGHT

Second floorplan of the Porchdog House. (Marlon Blackwell Architect)

care over the years and will last indefinitely compared to wood. The plain masonry blocks for the storage area can be left untreated.

As for sustainability, floors are covered in durable bamboo and operable windows encourage natural ventilation to reduce heating and cooling costs. Daylight streams in through windows on the east and west sides but can easily be controlled by opening or closing the shades for more or less light. Thanks to the durability of all the materials and the strength of the home's design, if and when another natural disaster such as Hurricane Katrina occurs, the home will be able to weather the storm. As Blackwell said, "The most sustainable thing about it is that after the next storm, the house will still be there."

The Porchdog House was completed in August 2009. It received a commendation from the Architectural Review for their 2010 House Awards and was shortlisted for the 2010 Brit Insurance Design Awards. For more than ten years Blackwell has been exploring the technologies that resulted in the Biloxi prototype of the Porchdog House, and hopefully more of these homes will be built in the future.

LEFT
A secure deck off the back serves as a second patio and industrial roll up garage door provides shade or security for the interior.

TOP RIGHT
The sides of the Metal shades drawn closed.

ABOVE
The lower staircase can handle being completely submerged from floodwaters.

NOTES

1 "Hurricane Katrina in the Gulf Coast: Mitigation Assessment Team Report, Building Performance Observations, Recommendations, and Technical Guidance." FEMA, July 2006.

TOP

Architect of the Porchdog House, Marlon Blackwell says "The most sustainable thing about it is that after the next storm, the house will still be there."

ABOVE

The durable and low maintenance home makes use of powder coated steel, masonry blocks, and metal screens.

PROJECT NAME
Silo Eco-Home

PROJECT YEAR
2010

LOCATION
Greensburg, Kansas, USA

PROJECT AREA
2,200 square feet

PROJECT TEAM
Greensburg GreenTown
(http://wwwgreensburggreentown.org)

APPROXIMATE COST
$275,000

ARCHITECT
Armour Homes
(http://www.armourh.com)

5.5

Silo Eco-Home

A tornado-proof home built green in Kansas serves as a model of disaster-proof design for hurricanes and severe weather.

On May 4, 2007, an EF5 tornado, 1.7 miles wide, ripped through the town of Greensburg, Kansas, leveling 95 percent of the city and killing twelve people in the process. One of the few buildings that remained standing was the grain elevator on the north side of town. Days later, as the citizens emerged from the rubble, they came together and decided to rebuild better and greener with the goal of a more sustainable city in terms of economy, the community, and the environment. The city council passed a resolution that all new buildings would be constructed to the USGBC LEED Platinum standard; Greensburg is the first city in the U.S. to make such a commitment.

From this town-wide resolution sprouted Greensburg GreenTown, a nonprofit organiza-tion led by Daniel Wallach devoted to helping the city incorporate sustainable principles into the rebuilding process. The organization has assisted with many projects, including starting a farmers' market, educational programs, a recycling pro-gram, a high school green club, and much more. In 2009, the organization began the Chain of Eco-Homes, a series of environmentally friendly demonstration homes to help educate the town's residents on green building strategies and serve as "living laboratories." Each home would be unique, be designed by a different architect, serve as eco-lodging for visitors to experience green liv-ing firsthand, and be monitored to learn how the technologies are performing.

Since the early 2000s, Dave Moffit of Armour Homes in Florida had been designing homes

OPPOSITE
The Silo Eco-Home serves as the offices for Greensburg Greentown organization as well as a bed and breakfast.

that were strong, durable, green, and affordable. His goal was to build homes that could survive a hurricane, fire, or tornado, last for centuries, be low maintenance, feature energy- and water-efficient design, and at the same time remain comparable to conventional housing in cost. Coincidentally, his latest design was a round concrete structure similar to that of the grain silo that had withstood the tornado's 205-mph winds. Watching the coverage of the disaster on TV, Moffit knew his design was perfect for Greensburg, so he contacted Wallach and offered up his design, the Silo Eco-Home, which became the first of the Chain of Eco-Homes. Currently, the home serves as Greensburg GreenTown's offices, Greensburg's Green Visitor Center, and a bed and breakfast.

Built using concrete construction techniques similar to those of the grain silo, the four-bedroom house, with its six-inch concrete walls and an arched concrete roof, is virtually indestructible. Armour has performed tests on the design, including loading the clearspan roof with 70,000 pounds of water and dropping a 2,000-pound car on the roof to simulate flying debris.

LEFT
Residents of Greensburg celebrate the opening of the Silo Eco-Home.

TOP RIGHT
The downstairs living room serves as a welcome center to visitors of Greensburg.

ABOVE
The home is full of non-toxic, natural, and environmentally friendly materials, many of which were donated by manufacturers.

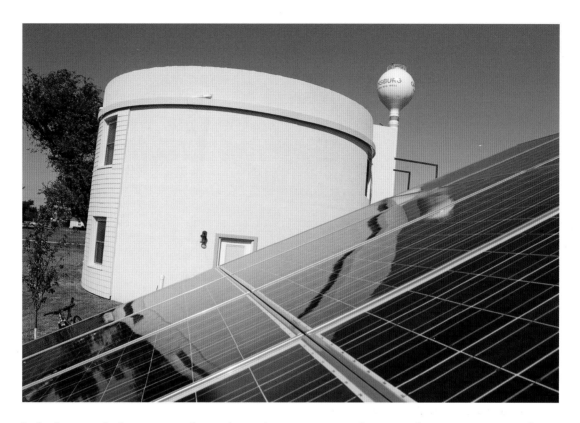

In both cases, the home was unharmed, proving that its structural integrity could survive the severest of storms, whether it were a tornado or a hurricane.

The compact home has a small footprint of about 1,000 square feet, and the round silo form reduces wind drag. The 6-inch-thick concrete walls, coupled with 4 inches of rigid EPS insulation, provide an R-value greater than 25, creating a tight, energy-efficient envelope and making the home very quiet even during storms. The arched concrete roof with no interior supports has an R-value of 40. Low-E windows are placed to optimize passive solar design. Energy-efficient LED and CFL lighting minimizes energy usage, while a 1.2 kW grid-tied photovoltaic system in the yard generates energy for the home. A home energy-monitoring system tracks energy production and energy usage, providing feedback on the home's energy performance.

Besides durability, the interior boasts a number of energy-efficient features and green materials and products, many of which were donated by manufacturers. Natural nontoxic, renewable, recycled, and reclaimed materials are used throughout, resulting in healthy indoor air quality. Outside, the home features a rainwater collection system, a rain garden, a permeable-pavement driveway, and a composting system. Native landscaping, the rainwater collection system, and the green rooftop garden, which were installed in the spring of 2011, all help absorb storm water.

A tornado shelter in the northeast corner of the house provides additional safety for employees and visitors. Designed foremost for durability and

ABOVE

A 1.2 kW grid tied photovoltaic system provides electricity for the house.

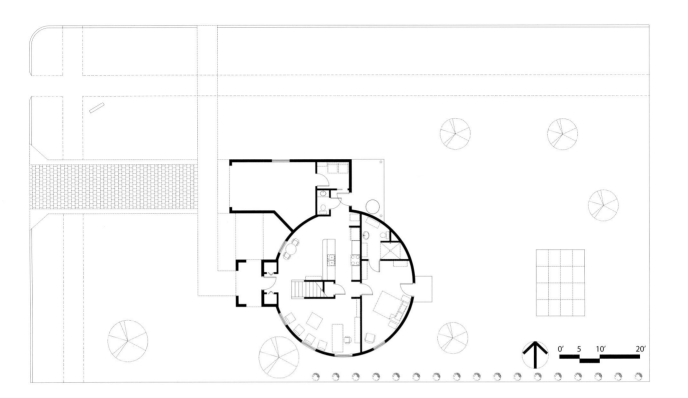

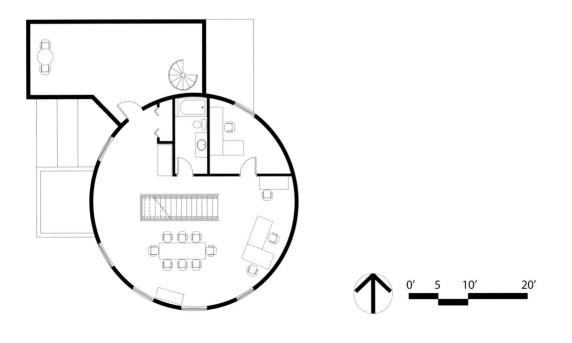

TOP

Ground floorplan of the Silo Eco-Home.

ABOVE

First floorplan of the Silo Eco-Home.

structural integrity, the Silo Eco-Home is certain to be around for a hundred years or more, even if subjected to severe storms such as the one that ripped through Greensburg in 2007. A home that can survive major storms is far more sustainable than one that must continually be rebuilt, and the Silo Eco-Home serves as an excellent example of disaster-proof design. Greensburg GreenTown is currently working on building more homes in their Chain of Eco-Homes and expects the next one to be completed in 2012. Armour Homes is continuing their research and design on durable, weatherproof homes and hopes to complete a hurricane-resistant home in the Grand Caymans by the end of 2011.

ABOVE
Visitors to the home check out the rooftop deck and the clearspan roof.

PROJECT NAME
Steigereiland 2.0

LOCATION
IJburg, Amsterdam,
The Netherlands

ARCHITECT
Faro Architecten
(http://www.faro.nl)

CONSTRUCTION ADVISOR
Pieters Bouwtechniek, Almere,
The Netherlands
(http://www.pieterbouwtechniek.nl)

SUSTAINABILITY ADVISOR
Trecodome
(http://www.trecodome.com)

CONSTRUCTION
J.J.A. Kerkhofs Montagebouw,
Hendrik-Ido-Ambacht

WINDOW SILLS AND PANELS
Woodworkers Overbeek,
Haaksbergen
(http://www.tifaoverbeek.nl)

HEATING INSTALLATIONS
Aitec & Wiessenekker, Rhenen
(http://www.aitec.nl)

PROJECT YEAR
2009

PROJECT AREA
2,475 square feet

APPROXIMATE COST
$ 693,604 (€550,000)

PHOTOS: I See For You / Föllmi Photography (unless otherwise indicated)

5.6

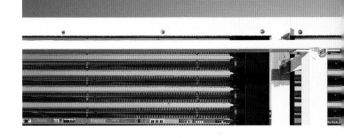

Steigereiland 2.0

A townhome in Amsterdam, designed to produce all of its own energy, serves as an example of how we can rebuild our urban environments in sustainable, energy-efficient ways.

With over 50 percent of the world's population living in urban areas, a number that is expected to grow to 70 percent by 2050, considerable focus for housing should be placed on urban solutions.[1] On top of that, most of the buildings and homes in urban areas are desperately in need of renovation and upgrades, especially in terms of energy efficiency and environmentally friendly materials. Whether renovated or torn down and built from scratch, the ideal goals for all urban dwellings should be to maximize their water and energy efficiency, utilize nontoxic and sustainable materials, and produce some or all of their own energy.

One such ideal urban home is Steigereiland 2.0 on IJburg Island in Amsterdam. Although a new construction on a recently created spit of land

in the water east of the city, the four-story home serves as an excellent example of sustainable and energy-efficient design in an urban environment. Dutch firm Faro Architecten designed the home for a couple who specifically wanted a net-zero residence, which includes the use of solar hot-water heating, a rooftop wind turbine, passive solar design, and a supertight envelope to minimize energy use.

The energy-neutral, three-bedroom residence sits among a long row of townhouses with narrow footprints that front the street and have small yards in back. The ground floor contains the entrance, kitchen, dining room, a bathroom, and access to the backyard. The second floor serves as a landing zone and small living space leading up to the private areas on the two upper floors,

---

OPPOSITE

Steigereiland 2.0 is a net zero home in IJburg, outside of Amsterdam.

ABOVE

An evacuated tube solar thermal hot water system heats water for radiant heating and domestic hot water.

233

where there are three bedrooms, two bathrooms, and an office.

The work of Japanese architect Terunobu Fuji-mori was a major source of inspiration for the design of the home, including the use of many natural elements such as trees, branches, and wood paneling. A large tree trunk, which was acquired from a nearby street when it was cut down, hangs above the ground floor and helps support the second-floor landing zone. The interior is completely finished in light-colored wood paneling. The exterior is almost the antithesis of the interior; it is clad in wood that has been charred on the outside to preserve it without the use of chemicals or paint. This traditional Japanese preservation method involves binding three boards together and lighting them from the bottom, but Faro found that charring the boards individually with a blowtorch produced a more even finish.

The home's envelope has tight joints, no thermal bridging, and thick organic insulation. All of the windows are triple paned and recessed into the façade to prevent excess sunlight from entering the home. Sunlight does provide thermal heating for the home in winter, but in summer, if too much sun enters, shades can be drawn to reduce the heat. A pergola in the backyard provides sun shading for the large ground-floor windows. The sun's energy is also used to heat a 105-square-foot solar thermal hot-water system located

on the roof. The system's evacuated tubes are installed vertically along the roof's edge almost like a railing, and the hot water they generate is used for all domestic needs. In addition, a rain-water harvesting system collects water from the roof and stores it in a cistern in the garden, so it can be used for irrigation and toilet flushing.

A ground source heat pump installed six feet below the ground provides heating and cooling for the home under the floor plane. Natural ventilation is encouraged by rooftop vents that help cool the home in summer, and heat exchangers maximize efficiency in winter. If extra heat is needed, a wood pellet stove can be lit. The home's tight envelope and energy-efficient systems ensure that very little heating or cooling escapes and very little energy is needed. For whatever energy is necessary, two grid-tied renewable energy systems on the rooftop supply it. A 1.5 kW donQi urban wind turbine mounted on the rooftop deck provides approximately a third of the home's energy; the remainder is produced by a photovoltaic system. When the two systems produce more energy than needed in the home, the electricity is shifted onto the grid. Likewise, when the owners use more energy than they are producing, they can take electricity from the grid.

LEFT

The four story home is a new construction, but serves as a great example for what can be done in urban settings.

RIGHT

A large tree trunk, acquired from a nearby street after it was cut down, hangs above the ground floor to support the second floor landing.

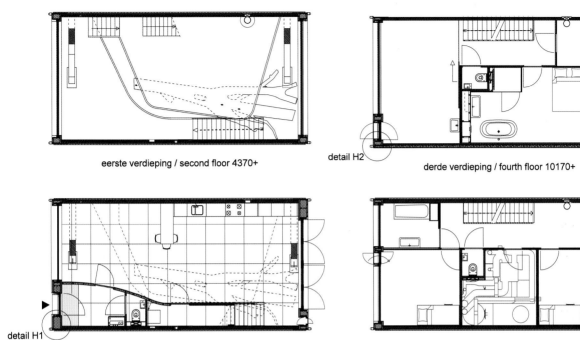

eerste verdieping / second floor 4370+

detail H2

derde verdieping / fourth floor 10170+

detail H1

begane grond / ground floor

tweede verdieping / third floor 7270+

Faro Architects used this home as a testing ground to explore all of the possibilities and techniques for sustainable urban building, and the result was an exceptionally energy-efficient home. Their use of renewable energy in the middle of a dense urban environment proves that it is not only possible but necessary for future development. Though the home was certainly expensive and built with high-end products and finishes, the research, systems, and building techniques developed in the design and construction of Steigereiland 2.0 will lead the way for lower-cost, energy-efficient urban housing.

NOTES

1   "Millennium Development Goals Report 2007." United Nations, New York, 2007. Accessed 8 March 2011, http://www.un.org/millenniumgoals/pdf/mdg2007.pdf.

TOP
Floorplans for Steigereiland 2.0. (FARO Architecten, The Netherlands)

RIGHT
The back of the home opens on to a small yard.

PROJECT NAME
Windcatcher House

LOCATION
Bluff, Utah, USA

PROJECT TEAM
Twenty-two Masters of Architecture
students from the University
of Colorado Denver
(http://www.ucdenver.edu)

PARTNER ORGANIZATION
Design Build Bluff
(http://www.designbuildbluff.org)

PROJECT YEAR
2010

PROJECT AREA
1,120 square feet

APPROXIMATE COST
$46,000 + donated materials

5.7

Windcatcher House

Architecture students from the University of Colorado design and build an energy-efficient, off-grid-capable home for a family in the Navajo Nation in southeastern Utah.

Design Build Bluff is a nonprofit organization with a two-fold mission. The first is to build energy-efficient and sustainable homes for people of the Navajo Nation in southeastern Utah. The second is to engage architecture students in a for-credit class not only to learn about another culture but also to design and build an entire home for a family. Between 2003, when the program began with students from the University of Utah, and 2010, seven homes were completed, all made from sustainable, salvaged, and recycled materials. Fundraising and grants from HUD supply about $50,000 per home, most of which goes to materials, although suppliers often donate materials. As the program is largely student run, labor to build the houses is entirely free, and the students spend an entire semester living and working out of the Bluff, Utah, base camp.

During the fall 2010 semester, twenty-two students from the College of Architecture and Planning at the University of Colorado Denver went to Bluff to build a home. They had spent the preceding summer selecting the family for whom their home would be built, as well as researching and designing it. The students chose Maxine Begay and her son, Maurice, as the recipients of the home, based on the Navajo Nation's assessment of need and eligibility. In total, the home took about thirteen weeks to construct, on a schedule of two weeks on and one week off, from September through December.

The Windcatcher House on the Navajo Nation in southern
Utah is built with rammed earth walls and features a wind
tower to provide cooling in the summer.

Begay was very much a part of the design process, and the students worked to incorporate her wishes and preferences into the home. Inspiration came from Navajo culture, but the design was also largely dependent on the desert climate of southern Utah. The private areas of the home—two bedrooms and a bathroom—are oriented to the east in line with Navajo tradition, which holds the morning light sacred. The public spaces, the kitchen and the dining and living room, are oriented to the west, where Begay's family's homes are located on the same plot of land. A flex space with a built-in loft bed can be turned into a guest room when her nephew comes to stay. Begay requested a spacious kitchen and wanted her home built up high enough to take advantage of the views and the breezes. Next to the home is a shaded structure for outdoor dining and socializing. Rainwater is collected on the roof and stored in a tank on the east side of the home; a trough on the west side provides drinking water for the horses and irrigation for the garden.

A narrow footprint, an east–west orientation, and lots of south-facing windows open the house up and maximize sunlight for passive heating in winter, while large roof overhangs protect the

---

TOP LEFT

22 University of Colorado Denver students designed and built the Windcatcher House in the Fall of 2010. (Mark Olsen)

TOP RIGHT

Detail of the many textures used to clad the exterior, including metal roof, salvaged rusty metal mesh, and cement board.

ABOVE LEFT

The bathroom features an eco resin shower divider made by 3Form and a sink fashioned from a dresser and handmade pottery.

ABOVE RIGHT

A large open kitchen features 3Form panels and concrete countertops.

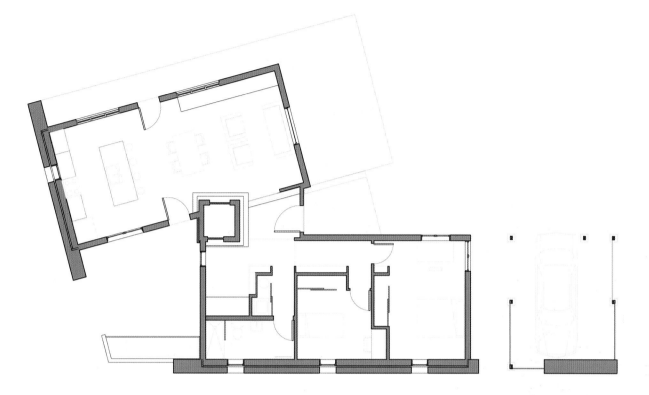

interior from the desert's hot summer sun. The south wall was constructed on site out of rammed earth for thermal mass, protection, and insulation. The north wall is stick frame, built with advanced framing techniques to conserve materials and clad in a custom cement board rainscreen system. The exposed-concrete floor rests on a frost-protected, shallow foundation, and the north-facing deck was constructed from donated cedar. Recycled denim was used for insulation in the roof and stick-frame walls, and the interior finishes include salvaged wood, reclaimed aluminum panels, salvaged metal, finish-grade plywood, custom concrete countertops, 3Form Ecoresin panels, and plastered gypsum board.

The centerpiece of the home is the Windcatcher, a thirty-foot-tall chimney-like structure in the center of the home that provides both cooling

and heating. In summer, metal panels over the fireplace are removed and the tower acts as an evaporative cooler. Breezes enter through the top and travel down over water-soaked pads to cool the incoming air. Operable clerestory windows encourage natural ventilation and the movement of the cool air throughout the home. Made of compressed earth blocks and insulated, the Windcatcher is closed down to stop the airflow in winter. An efficient wood stove incorporated into the Windcatcher and vented out the top provides heating in the colder months.

Many people in the Navajo Nation live too far from utilities to have electricity and must do without it. The students designed Begay's home to be off-grid capable and run completely on the energy generated by a photovoltaic system. Oriented to the south, the roof is optimally angled to

ABOVE

Floorplan of the Windcatcher House. (Mark Olsen)

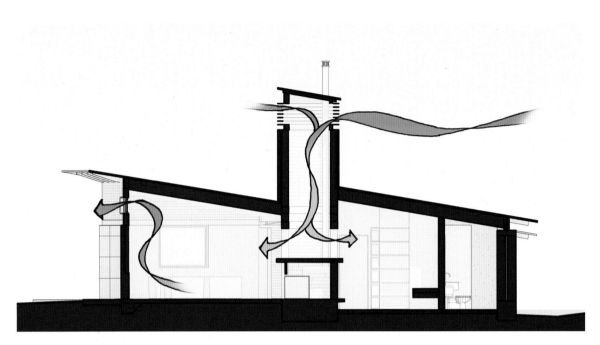

TOP

Diagram explaining the cooling mechanism
from the Windcatcher with the help of natural
ventilation. (Mark Olsen)

ABOVE

View of the Windcatcher House from the
southwest shows the back courtyard, a rainwater
fed trough and the garden. (Matt Meinhold)

maximize power generation. The PV system was not within the budget of the project, but luckily for the Begay family there are power and water utilities close to the site and Begay is only waiting for the Navajo Nation to install the connection. If funds become available for a PV system in the future, the home is energy efficient enough to require only a small one.

The Design Build Bluff program successfully serves its dual purpose as a provider of affordable housing and an educational program. Each semester a family of the Navajo Nation receives a low-maintenance, energy-efficient home that protects them from the harsh desert climate. The students walk away from the project with a greater understanding of the Native American culture and firsthand experience in the design and construction of a home. They also learn to appreciate how smart design can reduce a home's environmental impact, even to the point of being totally off grid. In 2011, Design Build Bluff became a year-round program with student groups from the University of Utah and the University of Colorado Denver participating and has the potential to construct up to four homes a year.

TOP LEFT

A salvaged tank was converted into a rainwater collecting system on the east side of the house. (Matt Meinhold)

TOP RIGHT

The hearth at the center of the home provides both heating and cooling. The panel above the fireplace can be removed to let in fresh air from the windcatcher.

ABOVE

View from the shade structure to the side door.

PROJECT NAME
Villa Vals
(http://www.villavals.ch)

LOCATION
Vals, Switzerland

ARCHITECTS
SeARCH (http://www.search.nl)
and CMA
(http://www.christian-muller.com)

DESIGN
Bjarne Mastenbroek and
Christian Müller

**INTERIOR CARDBOARD
ROOM DESIGN**
Studio JVM, Jeroen van Mechelen
(http://www.studiojvm.nl)

**CONTRACTOR MAIN
STRUCTURE**
Kurt Schnyder Bauunternehmung

**STRUCTURAL
ENGINEERING**
Alex Kilchmann

**GLASS FAÇADE ENGINEERING
AND CONSTRUCTION**
Walch GmbH

PROJECT YEAR
2009

PROJECT AREA
3,068 square feet

**APPROXIMATE
COST**
Undisclosed

5.8
Villa Vals

An unconventional yet practical home is built into the hillside of a Swiss mountain to preserve views and maximize energy efficiency.

In the Swiss mountain town of Vals there are many beautiful homes tucked into the alpine slopes to take advantage of the views and the famous thermal baths nearby. New construction is generally frowned upon, however, and proposals must always be weighed against their potential impact on the important tourist destination of the Therme Vals. A few years ago, a building site near the thermal baths became available, and the owner decided to take the chance of building an unusual home there. Rather than building a structure up from and out of the slope, the owner, with the help of architectural firms SeARCH and CMA, proposed building it within the slope. This approach proved acceptable to the city of Vals and also a way to achieve a high level of energy efficiency without disturbing the expansive views of the baths.

As a rule, building on steep slopes is not a wise practice, as it requires a strong foundation, sensible architecture, accurate engineering, and a lot of respect for the site. There is also the risk of avalanches or mud slides to contend with. In contrast, building in a steep slope can have some interesting benefits. Though there is certainly a considerable amount of earth to excavate and then fill back in during construction, the building is solidly encased in the ground, reducing risk of disaster. In addition, the relatively constant temperature of the earth tempers the indoor climate and increases overall energy efficiency. In the case of Villa Vals, the constant ground temperature helps keep the home warm in the winter, but the concept works equally well in hotter climates, where the earth serves to keep the home cool.

OPPOSITE

Villa Vals is an energy efficient home built into the side of a steep slope to minimize impact on its surroundings and neighbors' views.

ABOVE

Drawing of the home cut into the hillside.

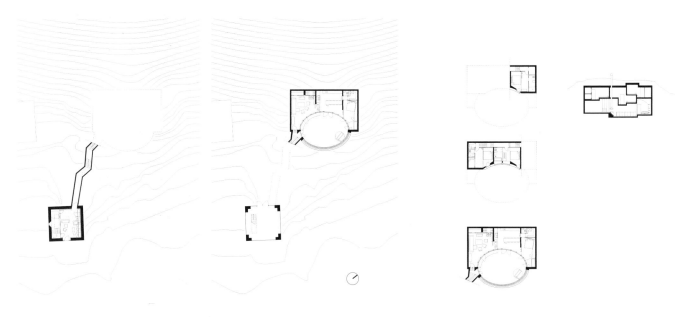

TOP

The constant temperatures of the earth help keep the interior climate more consistent.

ABOVE

Site plan and floorplans of Villa Vals.

Villa Vals is a compact, three-story home built into the steep slope around a central patio, creating one large, southeast-facing façade. From above, it looks as though a circular hole was cut from the earth and the home was inserted into it like a plug. Three stories of windows punctuate the front and overlook the large patio, which provides a sunny deck from which to take in the sights and enjoy the outdoors. The edge of the hole acts as a frame for the view, as though it were a painting. The home is accessed by entering a historic Graubünder barn in the front yard and ascending a staircase to a concrete underground tunnel that connects the two structures.

Inside, the first floor contains the kitchen, a large living space, a dining room, and a bedroom and bathroom decorated with whimsical shelving and

TOP LEFT
A concrete staircase leads to a bathroom on a raised platform.

ABOVE LEFT
Local stone and concrete act as thermal mass to soak up the sun's heat.

TOP RIGHT
Door to the underground tunnel leads right into the living room.

Gothic-style arches made out of cardboard. Various flights of stairs wind their way up through the house, rather like the underground tunnels of a burrowing animal. Bathrooms are elevated and beds are placed on raised platforms. Each room has a window that provides fantastic views and lots of natural daylight, all while soaking up the sunlight for passive heating.

Because the home is built into the ground, it generally remains at a more consistent temperature and is less affected by the weather than a traditional aboveground home. Villa Vals was largely constructed out of local materials using local labor. Concrete and local stone provide the thermal mass to soak up the sun's heat during the day and then release it slowly at night throughout the house. A geothermal heating and cooling system further improves energy efficiency. Air is

TOP

The home is accessed through a historic Graubünder barn and through an underground, concrete tunnel.

ABOVE RIGHT

Graising goats peer down from the slope into the home's courtyard.

brought in from outside and piped underground before entering the house. In the winter, the earth is warmer than the outside air, so the air in the home is preheated; in the summer, the earth is cooler, so it precools the indoor air. The large façade's fifteen triple-paned windows not only allow the sun to heat the interior but also provide insulation. The home sources its electricity from a local hydropower station, a renewable source of energy.

The home's underlying design principle was that it would fit in well with its environment, and Villa Vals' unique design is sensitive to its surroundings as well as to its neighbors because it has minimal impact on the views. Sheltered by the earth and protected from the elements, the home is highly energy efficient, thereby improving its sustainability. Earth-bermed or under-

ground homes are rising in popularity as a way to improve both energy efficiency and safety. Villa Vals' circular design is likely to influence a new wave of sustainable, underground homes, which will be much better equipped to handle extreme temperatures and severe weather than their aboveground counterparts. The intriguing home is not a full-time residence and is in fact available for vacation rental, providing an interesting opportunity to experience underground living firsthand.

ABOVE

This interesting underground home is available as a vacation rental.

ONLINE RESOURCES

Affordable Housing Institute: Organization devoted to building affordable and healthy housing communities worldwide. *(http://www.affordablehousinginstitute.org)*

Architecture for Humanity: Nonprofit dedicated to building a better future with the help of architecture and design professionals worldwide. *(http://architectureforhumanity.org)*

Disaster Research Center, University of Delaware: Research center devoted to the 150 social scientific study of disasters. *(http://www.udel.edu/DRC/index.html)*

EM-DAT The International Disaster Database: International database of global disasters, human impacts, disaster-related economic damage estimates, disaster-specific international aid contributions, and much more. *(http://www.emdat.be)*

Green Building Advisor: Online resource devoted to designing, building, and remodeling energy-efficient, sustainable, and healthy homes. *(http://www.greenbuildingadvisor.com)*

Habitat for Humanity: Global nonprofit dedicated to building simple, decent, and affordable housing for low-income families around the world. *(http://www.habitat.org)*

Inhabitat: Weblog devoted to green design, sustainable architecture, and tracking innovations in technology, techniques, and materials. *(http://www.inhabitat.com)*

Intergovernmental Panel on Climate Change: International scientific body tasked with reviewing and assessing the most recent scientific, technical, and socio-economic information regarding climate change around the world. *(http://www.ipcc.ch)*

International Federation of Red Cross and Red Crescent Societies: The world's largest humanitarian aid responder. *(http://www.ifrc.org)*

I-Rec Information and Research for Reconstruction: An international network focused on the study of reconstruction after disasters. *(http://www.grif.umontreal.ca/i-Rec.htm)*

Jetson Green: Weblog devoted to the design and construction of sustainable homes, natural materials, and green technology. *(http://www.jetsongreen.com)*

Open Architecture Network: An online, open source community dedicated to improving living conditions through innovative and sustainable design. Designers can share, collaborate, and manage design projects. *(http://openarchitecturenetwork.org)*

Oxfam International: International aid organization devoted to finding lasting solutions to poverty and injustice. *(http://www.oxfam.org)*

Plastic Sheeting: Information on the specification and use of plastic sheeting in humanitarian relief. *(http://plastic-sheeting.org)*

Prevention Web: An online information exchange for the disaster-risk-reduction community. *(http://www.preventionweb.net)*

Relief Web: Source for timely, reliable, and relevant humanitarian information and analysis. *(http://reliefweb.int)*

Shelter Centre: Swiss NGO that supports humanitarian aid organizations with strategic or policy guidelines, technical guidelines, and technical training, and serves as a global forum. *(http://sheltercentre.org)*

The Sphere Project: An initiative to define and uphold the standards by which the global community responds to the plight of people affected by disasters, principally through guidelines that are set out in the Humanitarian Charter and Minimum Standards in Disaster Response, known as the Sphere Handbook. *(http://www.sphereproject.org)*

UN-HABITAT: United Nations agency devoted to promoting socially and environmentally sustainable towns and cities with the goal of providing adequate shelter for all. *(http://www.unhabitat.org)*

United Nations International Strategy for Disaster Reduction: A strategic framework adopted by the United Nations' member states to reduce losses from disaster and build resilient nations and communities through sustainable development. *(http://www.unisdr.org)*

SELECTED BIBLIOGRAPHY

Abrams, Charles. *The Future of Housing*. New York: Harper & Brothers, 1946. Print.

Architecture for Humanity, Kate Stohr, and Cameron Sinclair. *Design like You Give a Damn: Architectural Responses to Humanitarian Crises*. New York: Metropolis Books, 2006. Print.

Architecture for Humanity. "Rebuilding 101 Manual: Rebuilding Strategies for Haiti." Open Architecture Network. Architecture for Humanity, March 2011. Web (http://openarchitecturenetwork.org/projects/rebuilding101).

Ashmore, Joseph, Jon Fowler, and James Kennedy. *Shelter Projects 2008: IASC Emergency Shelter Cluster*. UN-HABITAT, 2009. Web (http://www.unhabitat.org/pmss/listItemDetails.aspx?publicationID=2683).

Corsellis, Tom, and Antonella Vitale. *Shelter After Disaster: Strategies for Transitional Settlement and Reconstruction*. Isabelle De Muyser-Boucher. United Nations, Department for International Development, Shelter Centre, 2010. Web (http://sheltercentre.org/library/shelter-after-disaster).

Davis, Ian. *Shelter after Disaster*. Oxford, UK: Oxford Polytechnic, 1978. Print.

Interview with Bruce Wrightsman. Telephone interview, 17 December 2010.

Interview with Kenny Rae, Humanitarian Response Specialists, Oxfam America. Telephone interview, 14 December 2010.

Interview with Mario Flores, Habitat for Humanity. Telephone interview, 19 January 2011.

"IPCC 2007, Summary for Policymakers." In *Climate Change 2007: Impacts, Adaptation and Vulnerability. Contribution of Working Group II to the Fourth Assessment Report of the Intergovernmental Panel on Climate Change*. Cambridge, UK: Cambridge University Press, 2007. Print.

Jha, Abhas K., Jennifer Duyne Barenstein, Priscilla M. Phelps, Daniel Pittet, and Stephen Sena. *Safer Homes, Safer Communities: A Handbook for Reconstructing after Natural Disasters*. Washington, D.C.: World Bank, 2010.

Kousky, Carolyn, Olga Rostapshova, Michael Toman, and Richard Zeckhauser. "World Bank ELibrary Responding to Threats of Climate Change Mega-Catastrophes." World Bank ELibrary, November 2009. Web (http://elibrary.worldbank.org/content/workingpaper/10.1596/1813-9450-5127).

Lizarralde, Gonzalo, Cassidy Johnson, and Colin Davidson, eds. *Rebuilding after Disasters: From Emergency to Sustainability*. London: Spon Press, 2010. Print.

Magrath, John, Ian Bray, and Kim Scriven. "Climate Alarm: Disasters Increase as Climate Change Bites." Oxfam International, 23 November 2007. Web (http://www.oxfam.org/en/policy/bp108_climate_change_alarm_0711).

Maplecroft. "Climate Change Vulnerability Index (CCVI)." Maplecroft | Global Risks Portfolio, 21 October 2010. Web (http://www.maplecroft.com/about/news/ccvi.html).

Office of the United Nations Disaster Relief Co-Ordinator. *Shelter After Disaster: Guidelines for Assistance*. New York: United Nations, 1982. Print.

Planning Sustainable Cities: Global Report on Human Settlements 2009. UN-HABITAT, 2009. Print and Web (http://www.unhabitat.org/content.asp?typeid=19&catid=555&cid=5607).

Smith, Peter F. *Building for a Changing Climate: The Challenge for Construction, Planning and Energy*. London: Routledge, 2009. Print.

United Nations International Strategy for Disaster Reduction. *Global Assessment Report on Disaster Risk Reduction: Summary and Recommendations (2009)*.

United Nations, 2009. Web (http://www.preventionweb.net/english/hyogo/gar/report/index.php?id=9413).

INDEX